SOWING
AND
REAPING

SOWING
AND
REAPING

*Whatever a man sows that shall
he also reap.* (Galatians 6:7)

D. L. Moody

ANEKO
PRESS

We love hearing from our readers. Please contact us at www.anekopress.com/questions-comments with any questions, comments, or suggestions.

Sowing and Reaping – Dwight L. Moody

Revisions Copyright © 2019

First edition published 1896

Originally published by Fleming H. Revell Company, Chicago; New York; Toronto

Cover Design: J. Martin

Cover Photography: SeDmi/Shutterstock

Editor: Paul Miller

Printed in the United States of America

Aneko Press

www.anekopress.com

Aneko Press, Life Sentence Publishing, and our logos are trademarks of

Life Sentence Publishing, Inc.
203 E. Birch Street
P.O. Box 652
Abbotsford, WI 54405

RELIGION / Christian Life / Spiritual Growth

Paperback ISBN: 978-1-62245-637-6

eBook ISBN: 978-1-62245-638-3

10 9 8 7 6 5 4 3 2

Available where books are sold

Contents

Chapter 1

Sowing and Reaping

Do not deceive yourselves; God is not mocked: for whatever a man sows that shall he also reap. For he that sows to his flesh shall of the flesh reap corruption, but he that sows in the Spirit shall of the Spirit reap eternal life. (Galatians 6:7-8)

I think the above passage contains truths that no unbeliever or skeptic will dare to deny. There are some passages in the Word of God that do not need any other proof than that which we can easily find in our daily experience. This is one of them. Even if the Bible were to be blotted out of existence, the words in the verses above would be abundantly verified by what is constantly happening around us. We only have to look at the news to see them being fulfilled before our eyes.

I remember reading this text once when a man stood right up in the audience and said, "I don't believe it."

I said, "My friend, that doesn't change the fact that truth is truth whether you believe it or not, and a lie is a lie whether you believe it or not."

He didn't want to believe it. When the meeting broke up, an officer was at the door to arrest him. He was tried and sent to the penitentiary for twelve months for stealing. I suspect that when he got into his cell, he believed that he had to reap what he sowed.

We might as well try to blot the sun out of the heavens as to blot this truth out of the Word of God. It is heaven's eternal decree. This law has been enforced for six thousand years. Did not God make Adam reap what he sowed even before he left Eden? Did not Cain reap outside of Eden? Everyone must reap what he sows, whether he is a king on the throne, like David, or a priest behind the altar, like Eli.

Everyone must reap what he sows, whether he is a king on the throne, like David, or a priest behind the altar, like Eli.

Priest and prophet, preacher and hearer – all must reap what they sow. I believed it ten years ago, but I believe it a hundred times more today.

My text applies to the individual, whether he is a saint, a sinner, or a hypocrite who thinks he is a saint. It applies to the family, to society, and to nations. The law that the result of actions must be reaped is as true for nations as for individuals. Indeed, someone has said that as nations have no future existence, this world is the only place to punish them as nations. See how God has dealt with them. See if they have not reaped what they sowed. Take Amalek: *Remember what Amalek did unto thee by the way when ye were come forth out of Egypt, how he met thee by the way and smote the hindmost of thee, even all that were feeble behind thee, when thou wast faint and weary and he did not fear God* (Deuteronomy 25:17-18). What was to be the result of this attack? Was it to go unpunished? God ordained that Amalek should reap as he sowed, and the nation was all but wiped out of existence under King Saul.

What has become of the monarchies and empires of the world? What brought ruin on Babylon? Her king and people would not obey God, and ruin came upon them. What has become of Greece and all her power? She once ruled the world. What has become of Rome and all her greatness? When her cup of iniquity was full, it was dashed to the ground. What happened to the Jews? They rejected salvation, persecuted God's messengers, and crucified their Redeemer – and we find that more than a million of them perished at one time.

Look at the history of this country. Despite an open Bible, our forefathers allowed slavery, but judgment came at last. There was hardly a family in the North or in the South that did not have to mourn over someone taken from them.

Take the case of France. It is said that a century ago people were spending millions of dollars every year in France in the publication and distribution of literature that was contrary to biblical principles and Christianity. What has been the harvest? Has France not reaped? Notice the result: The Bible was suppressed. God was denied. Hell broke loose. More than a million people were beheaded, shot, drowned, or put to death some other way between September 1792 and December 1795. Since then, France has had thirteen revolutions in eighty years, and there has been a turnover in government on an average of once every nine months. One-third of the births in Paris are illegitimate. Ten thousand newborn infants have been fished out at the outlet of the city sewers in a single year. The native population of France is decreasing. The percentage of suicides is greater in Paris than in any city in the West. Since the French Revolution, there have been enough French men and women slaughtered in the streets of Paris in the various insurrections to average more than twenty-five hundred each year!

The principle was not new in Scripture or in history when Paul expressed it in his letter to the Galatians. Paul clothed it in common, simple language, but to dress it up we could say that the law of sowing and reaping is the law of cause and effect, the law of retribution or retaliation, and the law of compensation. It is not my purpose to enter now into a philosophical discussion of the law as it appears under any of these names. We see that it exists. It is beyond reasonable dispute. Whatever else skeptics may find fault with and criticize in the Bible, they must acknowledge this truth. It does not depend upon revelation for its support. Philosophers are in agreement with it as much as they are in agreement with anything.

The Supremacy of Law

The objection might be made, though, that while this

law of reaping and sowing can be applied to the physical world, it is not so certain in the spiritual realm. It is specifically here that modern research steps in. The laws of the spiritual world have been largely identified as the same laws that exist in the natural world. Indeed, it is claimed that the spiritual existed first, that the natural came after, and that when God proceeded to frame the universe, He followed the pattern that He already laid down.

Basically, God sent the higher laws downward so that the natural world became an incarnation, a visible representation, a working model of the supernatural. In the spiritual world, the same wheels work – without the iron.

> The evil harvest of sin and the good harvest of righteousness are as sure to follow the sowing as the harvest of wheat and barley.

Our whole life is thus bound and governed by laws ordained and established by God, and a person reaping what he sows is a law that can be easily observed and verified, whether we are talking about sowing to the flesh or sowing to the Spirit. The evil harvest of sin and the good harvest of righteousness are as sure to follow the sowing as the harvest of wheat and barley.

Life Is Not Casual, but Causal

As we continue, we will see that this law was in effect in the earliest periods of Bible history. Job's three friends reasoned that Job must be a significant sinner, because they took it for granted that the tragedies that happened to him must have been the result of his wickedness. Job's friend Eliphaz said, *Remember, I pray thee, who ever perished, being innocent? Or where were the righteous cut off? Even as I have seen, those that plow iniquity and sow wickedness, reap the same* (Job 4:7-8).

In the book of Proverbs we find it written, *The wicked works a deceitful work, but to him that sows righteousness shall be a sure reward* (Proverbs 11:18), and *He that sows iniquity shall reap iniquity* (Proverbs 22:8).

In Isaiah we find these words: *Say unto the righteous that it shall be well with him, for they shall eat of the fruit of their doings. Woe unto the wicked! It shall be ill with him, for according to the work of his hands it shall be done unto him* (Isaiah 3:10-11).

Hosea prophesied regarding Israel, *They have sown the wind, and they shall reap the whirlwind* (Hosea 8:7). Then he advised them, *Sow yourselves unto righteousness, reap yourselves unto mercy* (Hosea 10:12).

Teaching from Analogy

The Bible is full of analogies drawn from nature. When Christ was on earth, His favorite mode of teaching was to convey heavenly truths in earthly attire.

> Truths came forth from His lips, not stated simply on authority, but based on the analogy of the universe. His human mind, in perfect harmony with the divine mind with which it was united, discerned the connection of things and read the eternal will in

the simplest laws of nature. For instance,
if it were a question of whether God would
give His Spirit to those who asked, it was not
replied to by a truth revealed on His authority; the answer was derived from facts lying
open to all men's observation: "Behold the
fowls of the air"; "Behold the lilies of the
field" – learn from them the answer to your
question. A principle was there. God sup-
plies the needs that He has created. He feeds
the ravens. He clothes the lilies. He will feed
with His Spirit the craving spirits of His
children.[1]

This is the style of teaching that Paul adopts in the text.
He takes the simple process of sowing and reaping, a
process familiar to all, and finds in it a deeply spiritual
and moral meaning. It is as if he said that every person
scatters seed at every step as he journeys through life.
The seed consists of his thoughts, words, and actions.
They pass from him, and in time (it may be sooner or
later), they spring up and bear fruit, and the reaping
time comes.

Life Is a Seedtime

This analogy contains some serious lessons. Life is to
be regarded as a seedtime. Everyone has a field to sow,

---

[1]   From a sermon called "The Principle of Spiritual Harvest," preached
by English pastor Frederick W. Robertson (1816-1853) on December
15, 1849. One interesting note about Robertson was that he memo-
rized the entire New Testament in both English and Greek.

to cultivate, and finally, to reap. We are cultivating the seed for the coming harvest by our habits, by our interaction with friends and companions, and by exposing ourselves to good or bad influences. We cannot see the seed as it grows and develops, but time will reveal it.

Just as the full-grown harvest is potentially contained in the seed, so the full results of sin or holiness are potentially contained in the sinful or holy deed. *When lust has conceived, it brings forth sin; and sin, when it is finished, brings forth death* (James 1:15).

Just as we cannot reap a good harvest unless we have sown good seed, so we cannot reap eternal life unless we have sown to the Spirit. Weeds are easy to grow. They grow without being planted, and sin springs up naturally in the human heart. Ever since our first parents broke away from God, the human heart has of itself been thoroughly vile, and all its fruits have been evil. *The heart of the sons of men is fully set in them to do evil* (Ecclesiastes 8:11). Do you doubt it? If you do, ask yourself what would become of a child if he was left to himself with no training, no guidance, and no education. In spite of all that is done for children, the evil too often gets the upper hand. The good seed must be planted and cared for, often with toil and trouble, but the harvest will be certain.

> We cannot see the seed as it grows and develops, but time will reveal it.

Do we desire the love of our fellow men in our seasons of trial? Then we must love them when they need its cheering influence most. Do we long for sympathy in our sorrow and pain? We will have it if we weep with those who are weeping (Romans 12:15). Do we hope to reap eternal life? Then we must not sow to the flesh, or we will reap corruption. Rather, we must sow to the Spirit, and then the promise is that we will reap its immortal fruits.

Dr. Thomas Chalmers has drawn attention to the difference between the act of sowing and the act of reaping:

> Let it be observed that the act of indulging in the desires of the flesh is one thing, while the act of providing for the indulgence of them is another. When a man, on the impulse of sudden provocation, wreaks his resentful feelings upon the neighbor who has offended him, he is not at that time preparing for the indulgence of a carnal feeling, but is actually indulging it. He is not at that time sowing, but is reaping (such as it is) a harvest of gratification. This distinction may serve to assist our judgment in estimating the ungodliness of certain people.

> Rambling pleasure seekers who are carried along by every impulse, and all those whose powers of mental discipline are so enfeebled that they have become slaves of every propensity, live in the perpetual harvest of criminal gratification.

> A daughter whose sole delight is in her rapid transitions from one scene of worldly show

to another, who consumes every care and fills every hour with the frivolities and fascinations of her unstable society – she leads a life of which nothing can be imagined that is more opposite to a life of preparation for the coming judgment or the coming eternity; yet she reaps rather than sows.

Someone else gathers the money that purchases all things, and she tastes the fruits of the purchase. It is the father who sows. It is he who is busy and anxious over his speculations, wrinkled, perhaps, by care, and made solemn by years into an utter distaste for the splendors and insignificances of fashionable life.

The father sows, and he reaps in his daughter's life.

Painting for Eternity

Apelles, a Greek artist, was well known for the careful manner in which he went about his work. When someone asked him why he took such great care, he replied, "Because I am painting for eternity."

It is a solemn thing to think that the future will be the harvest of the present – that my condition in my dying hour may depend upon my actions today! Belief in a future life and in a coming judgment magnifies the importance of the present. Eternal issues depend upon it. The opportunity for sowing will not last forever; it is slipping through our fingers moment by moment, and the future can only reveal the harvest of the seed sown now.

A sculptor once showed a visitor his studio. It was full of statues of gods. One was rather interesting. The face was concealed by hair, and there were wings on each foot.

"What is his name?" asked the visitor.

"Opportunity," was the reply.

"Why is his face hidden?"

"Because people seldom know him when he comes to them."

"Why does he have wings on his feet?"

"Because he is soon gone, and once he is gone, he can never be overtaken."

It is wise for us to make the most of the opportunities God has given us. It depends a good deal on ourselves as to what our future will be. We can sow for a good harvest, or we can do like the Sioux Indians did, who once, when the United States Commissioner of Indian Affairs sent them a supply of grain for planting, ate it up. People are constantly sacrificing their eternal future to the passing enjoyment of the present moment. They fail or neglect to recognize the dependence of the future upon the present.

> People are constantly sacrificing their eternal future to the passing enjoyment of the present moment.

Everything We Do Matters

We can learn from this that there is no such thing as a wasted moment on earth. When we realize that every thought, word, and action has an eternal influence and will come back to us in the same way as the seed returns in the harvest, we must understand the responsibility of each thought, word, and action, however unimportant they may seem at the moment. We tend to overlook the results that hinge on small things. The law of gravitation was suggested by the fall of an apple. It is said that some years ago a Harvard professor brought some gypsy moths to this country in the hope that they could advantageously be crossed with silkworms. The moths accidentally got away and multiplied so enormously that the Commonwealth of Massachusetts had to spend hundreds of thousands of dollars trying to exterminate them.

When Henry Stanley was making his way through the forests of darkest Africa, the most formidable foes that he encountered, those who caused the most loss of life to his caravan and came the nearest to entirely defeating his expedition, were the little men of the Wambutti tribe. They hindered his expedition so much that only very slow progress could be made through the areas where they lived.

These little men only had little bows and little arrows that looked like children's toys, but upon these tiny arrows was a small drop of poison that would kill an elephant or a man as quickly and as surely as a Winchester rifle. Their defense was by means of poison and traps. They would slip through the darkness of the forest and, waiting in ambush, let fly their deadly arrows before they could be discovered. They dug ditches and carefully covered them over with leaves. They fixed spikes in the ground, tipped them with deadly poison, and then covered them. Into these ditches and on these spikes man and beast would fall or step to their death.

A lady once writing to a young man in the navy who was practically a stranger, thought, *Should I end this letter as most people would, or should I say a word for my Master?* Lifting up her heart for a moment, she wrote and told him that his constant change of scenery and location was an apt illustration of the word, *Here we have no continuing city, but we seek the one that is coming* (Hebrews 13:14). Trembling, she folded it and sent it off.

Back came the answer: "Thank you so much for those kind words! I am an orphan, and no one has spoken to me like that since my mother died many years ago." The arrow hit home, and the young man soon after rejoiced in the fullness of the blessing of the gospel of peace.

An obscure man preached one Sunday to a few people in a Methodist chapel in the south of England. A fifteen-year-old boy was in the audience, driven into the chapel by a snowstorm. The man took as his text the words, *Look unto me, and be ye saved* (Isaiah 45:22). As the preacher stumbled along as best he could, the light of heaven flashed into that boy's heart. He went out of the chapel saved, and soon became known as C.

H. Spurgeon, the boy preacher, who went on to influence millions of people with the gospel of Jesus Christ.

The parsonage at Epworth, England, caught fire one night, and all who lived there had been rescued except for one son. The boy went to a window and was brought safely to the ground by two farmhands, one standing on the shoulder of the other. The boy was John Wesley. If you want to realize the importance of that incident, if you want to measure the consequences of that rescue, just ask the millions of Methodists who look to John Wesley as the founder of their denomination.

Chapter 2

Be Not Deceived: God Is Not Mocked

Let no one deceive you. (Ephesians 5:6)

As one man mocks another, do ye so mock him? (Job 13:9)

We have all lived long enough to know what it is to be deceived. We have been deceived by our friends, by our enemies, by our neighbors, and by our relatives. Ungodly companions have deceived us. At every turn of life, we have been imposed upon in one way or another.

False teachers have crossed our paths, and under pretense of doing us good, have poisoned our minds with error. They have held out hopes to us that have proved false. They were apples of Sodom – fair on the outside, but full of ashes within. They have told us that there is no God, no future life, and no judgment to come. They have said that all people will be saved, that there is plenty of time to repent, and that we can be saved by doing the best we can.

Sin has deceived us. Every sinner is under a delusion. Sin meets him cheerfully and offers him pleasures and delights that are not pure and lasting.

During our meetings in Boston, a young man entered the tabernacle. He looked around and thought to himself that the people who went there – those who had businesses, comfortable homes, and good clothes – were great fools. This man had nothing in the world; he was a tramp and had come in there to keep himself warm, but to think that people who had homes would come and spend their time listening to such things as I preached was more than he could understand.

After he had been coming there for two weeks, I happened to point right down to where he was sitting one night, and I said, "Young man, be not deceived!" God used that as an arrow to his heart. He began to think about himself. His mind went back to the time when he had a good situation in Boston, when he was a young man making a good living, when he had a comfortable life and had many friends.

Then he looked at his present condition. His friends were all gone, his clothes were gone, his money was gone, and there he was – an outcast in that city. He said to himself, *I have been deceived*, and that very hour God woke him. He wanted to get friends to pray for him, but as he was not able to buy a piece of paper or pay for a postage stamp, he got an old piece of dirty paper, stood up in the street, and wrote a request to be read in the tabernacle. His request was that if God would save a poor, lost man like him, he wanted to be saved. His prayer was answered. As in the case of Nebuchadnezzar, his friends gathered around him again and the Lord restored him to position and to society. His eyes were opened to see how he had been deceived.

Satan

How many people all over the world are being deceived by the god of this world! It has been claimed that during the late Franco-German war, German drummers and trumpeters used to give the French beats and calls in order to deceive their enemies. The command to "halt" or "cease firing" was often given by the Germans, it has been said, and the French soldiers were thus placed in positions where they could be shot down like cattle.

Satan is the archenemy of our souls, and he has often blinded our reason and deceived our conscience by his lies and deception. He has often come as *an angel of light* (2 Corinthians 11:14), concealing his hideousness under a borrowed disguise. He says to a young man, "Sow your wild oats. There is time enough to turn to Christ after you grow old."

> Satan promises great things to his victims in the indulgence of their lusts, but they never realize the promises.

The young man yields himself to a life of indulgence and selfish desires under the false hope that he will obtain satisfaction, and it will be good if he awakens to the deception before his appetites become tyrants, dragging him down into depths of want and woe. Satan promises great things to his victims in the indulgence of their lusts, but they never realize the promises. The promised pleasure turns out to be pain, the promised heaven a hell.

Beware lest Satan deceives you as he deceived Eve in the beginning. *There is no truth in him. When he speaks a lie, he speaks of his own, for he is a liar and the father of it* (John 8:44).

Our Hearts

We have been deceived by our own hearts most of all. We have all proved the truth of this Bible verse: *The heart is deceitful above all things and desperately wicked; who shall know it?* (Jeremiah 17:9). How many times we have said that we would never do a certain thing again, and then have done it within twenty-four hours! A person may think he has reached its depths, but he finds there are further depths he has not reached. What absolute self-deception is due to it! *He that trusts in his own heart is a fool*, said Solomon (Proverbs 28:26). Martin Luther once said that he feared his own heart more than the pope and all the cardinals.

Many weeping wives have come to me about their husbands, saying, "He is good at heart." The truth is that his heart is the worst spot in him. If the heart was good, all else would be right. Out of the heart are the issues of life (Proverbs 4:23). Jesus said, *From within,*

> We have been deceived by our own hearts most of all.

out of the heart of men, come forth the evil thoughts, the adulteries, the fornications, the murders, the thefts, the covetousness, the wickedness, the deceit, the lasciviousness, the evil eye, the slander, the pride, the unwiseness (Mark 7:21-22). That is Christ's own statement regarding the unregenerate heart.

Some years ago, a remarkable picture was exhibited in London. As you looked at it from a distance, you seemed to see a monk engaged in prayer with his hands clasped and his head bowed. As you got nearer and examined the painting more closely, though, you saw that he was really squeezing a lemon into a punchbowl! What a picture that is of the human heart! Superficially examined, the heart is thought to be the seat of all that is good and noble and pleasing in a person, but in reality, until regenerated by the Holy Spirit, it is the seat of all corruption. *This is the condemnation, that the light is come into the world, and men loved darkness more than the light because their deeds were evil* (John 3:19).

A Jewish rabbi once asked his scholars what the best thing was that a man could have in order to keep him on the straight path. One scholar said that a good disposition was the best thing, another said it was a good companion, and another said that wisdom was the best thing he could desire. At last a scholar replied that he thought a good heart was best of all.

"True," said the rabbi. "You have comprehended all that the others have said. For he who has a good heart will have a good disposition and will be a good companion and a wise man. Let everyone, therefore, cultivate sincerity and uprightness of heart at all times, and it will save him an abundance of sorrow." We need to pray the prayer of David: *Create in me a clean heart, O God, and renew a right spirit within me* (Psalm 51:10).

God Is Not Mocked

Bear in mind that the God of the Bible has never deceived anyone, never can deceive anyone, and never will deceive anyone. That is the difference between the God of the Bible and the god of this world. The God of the Bible sees and knows the ways of men. He looks into their hearts. He knows their secret ways. They do not need to try to tell Him their secrets or try to conceal anything from Him.

No matter how successfully we might deceive or be deceived by ourselves or others, we cannot deceive God. Adam and Eve tried it in Eden when they hid themselves from the presence of Jehovah among the trees of the garden (Genesis 3:8). Saul tried it when he spared the best of the sheep and oxen of the Amalekites under the pretense of sacrificing them to God (1 Samuel 15). Ananias and Sapphira tried it when they lied about keeping back part of the price of the land they sold. Peter said to Ananias, *Why has Satan filled thy heart to lie to the Holy Spirit and to defraud of the price of the land? Retaining it, was it not thy own? and after it was sold, was it not in thine own power? Why hast thou conceived this thing in thy heart? Thou hast not lied unto men, but unto God* (Acts 5:3-4).

People try it every day. For some reason they think that God can be mocked. Because they can deceive their pastor, their employer, and their friends, they think they can deceive God. They put on false appearances, use empty words, perform unreal service, make idle excuses, and indulge in all kinds of hypocrisy, but it is of no avail. God cannot be deceived. He sees the corruption inside the whited sepulchre.

Warning to Christians

It is worth noticing that Paul gave this warning to Christians – converts in the Galatian church. After all, a person is not deceived all the time about his sins. The drunkard realizes in his sober moments what the result will be if he continues in his life of alcohol. Loss of self-respect and of the esteem of friends, the symptoms he soon begins to bear in his body, such as unsteady hands and discolored features – these things are the quick harvest of drunkenness and can easily be detected as they ripen. The immoral person often reaps the early fruit of his sin in diseases of the body, which are often effective warnings against continuing on such a dangerous path. But with "respectable" sins it is different. A person may be sowing for years and not even realize it himself.

You remember that in the parable of the sower, some seeds fell among thorns, and the thorns sprung up and choked them. Our Master, expounding this parable, said, *He that was planted among the thorns is he that hears the word, and the cares of this world and the deceitfulness of riches choke the word, and he becomes unfruitful* (Matthew 13:22). Who would have expected that this would be the result of the world or of riches? It has been said that Christ never spoke of riches except in words of warning. We do not tend to regard them that way today. People are trampling each other down in the pursuit of wealth. *Be not deceived.* He who sets his heart upon money is sowing to the flesh and will of the flesh reap corruption. "Adversity hath slain her thousand, but prosperity her ten thousand."[2]

"What is the value of this estate?" said one gentleman to another as they passed a fine mansion surrounded by fair and fertile fields.

"I don't know what it is valued at, but I know what it cost its late possessor."

"How much?"

"His soul."

An English clergyman was called to the deathbed of a wealthy parishioner. Kneeling beside the dying man, the pastor asked him to take his hand as he prayed for his strength in that solemn hour, but he declined to give the pastor his hand. After the end had come and they turned down the covers, the rigid hands were found holding the key to the man's safe in their death grip. His heart and hand had clung to his possessions to the very end, but he could not take them with him.

A person can be proud, and his very sin can be considered a virtue by some men. Hear what the Word of God says: *A high look and a proud heart . . . is sin*

---

2   This quote is from the book, *Precious Remedies against Satan's Devices*, written by the non-conformist Puritan pastor and author, Thomas Brooks (1608-1680). The quote is similar to 1 Samuel 18:7: *Saul has slain his thousands and David his ten thousands.*

(Proverbs 21:4), and *Every one that is proud in heart is an abomination to the Lord* (Proverbs 16:5).

These are the mistakes people make. They are leading respectable lives, and they think all is well. They do not recognize the stain of corruption upon many of the most cherished objects of their hearts. Those who profess to be Christians need to especially beware that they are not being deceived.

Neglect

How careful people should be of their thoughts, practices, and feelings! The reason for deception is, for the most part, neglect. People do not stop to examine themselves, to open their hearts and minds as in the sight of God, and to judge themselves by His most holy will. A person does not need to shoot himself in order to commit suicide; he only needs to neglect the proper means of sustenance, and he will soon die. Where an enemy is strong and aggressive, an army is doomed to certain defeat and capture unless a sharp lookout is kept, with every person wide awake at his post of duty.

> Those who profess to be Christians need to especially beware that they are not being deceived.

It has been noticed that there are more accidents in Switzerland in pleasant seasons than in stormy ones. People are apt to undertake expeditions that they would not take under less favorable conditions, and they are less careful in their conduct. In the same way, moral and spiritual disaster usually overtakes people when they are not guarding their hearts and when they are careless against temptation. They become proud and self-reliant in seasons of prosperity, whereas adversity drives them to the living God for guidance and comfort.

Dr. Samuel Johnson once said that the reason for so much deception and untruthfulness in the world is more from carelessness regarding the truth than from intentional lying, and therefore there is a great necessity for continual watchfulness. The Persians had an annual festival when they slew all the serpents and venomous creatures they could find, but then they allowed them to swarm as fast and freely as ever until the festival came around once more. It was poor policy. Sins, like serpents, breed quickly and need to be constantly watched.

We ought to watch on every side, too. Many people have fallen at the very point where they thought they were the safest. The meekness of Moses has become a proverb, yet he lost the promised land because he allowed the children of Israel to provoke him, and he spoke unadvisedly with his lips. Peter was the most zealous and defiant of the disciples, bold and outspoken, yet he degenerated for a short time into a lying, swearing, sneaking coward, afraid of a maid.

There is an old fable that a doe with only one eye used to graze near the sea. In order to be safe, she kept her blind eye toward the water, from which side she expected no danger, while with the good eye she watched the country. Some men, perceiving this, took a boat and came upon her from the sea and shot her. With her dying breath, she said, "Oh! What a difficult fate, that I should receive my death wound from that side where I expected no harm, and was safe in the part where I looked for most danger."

Let danger and need drive you closer to God. He never slumbers or sleeps (Psalm 121:4), and you will be safe in His keeping. Seize hold of Him in prayer. *Watch and pray* (Matthew 26:41).

Christianity Not Responsible for Deception

Christianity is not responsible for the deception that exists among its professing disciples. The illustration has been used before that you might just as reasonably hold the Cunard cruise ship company responsible for the suicide of a passenger who jumps overboard from one of their vessels at sea. If the person had remained on the vessel, he would have been safe, and if the disciple had remained true to his principles, he never would have turned out to be a hypocrite.

Was anybody ever more severe in denouncing hypocrisy than Jesus Christ? Do you want to know the reason why the church is scandalized every now and then by the exposure of some leading church member or even the pastor? It is not because of his Christianity, but it is because of his lack of it. Some secret sin has been eating at the heart of the tree, and in a critical moment it is blown down and its rottenness is revealed.

The Deception Cannot Last Forever

It is impossible for the deception to last forever. Abraham

Lincoln had a saying that you may be able to deceive all the people some of the time, and some of the people all of the time, but you will not be able to deceive all the people all of the time. Death will uncover the deception if it has not been detected sooner, and the unfortunate victim will stand, undeceived, in the presence of a God who cannot be mocked.

Chapter 3

When a Man Sows, He Expects to Reap

Behold, the husbandman waits for the precious fruit of the earth, waiting patiently until it receives the early and latter rain. (James 5:7)

Notice these four things about sowing and reaping:

1. A person expects to reap when he sows.

2. He expects to reap the same kind of seed that he sows.

3. He expects to reap more than he sows.

4. Ignorance of the kind of seed makes no difference.

First, when a person sows, he expects to reap. If a farmer went on planting spring after spring and never reaping in the autumn, you might say that he was not very wise at all, and might just be insane. Instead, a good farmer is always looking forward to the time when he will reap the reward of his toil. He never expects that the seed he has sown will be lost.

A young person who serves a long apprenticeship to some trade or profession expects to eventually reap the fruit of all those years of patient hard work and training. Ask an engineer why he works so hard for five, six, or seven years in the endeavor to learn his profession. He replies that he is looking forward to the reaping time, when his fortune and reputation will be earned. The lawyer studies long and hard, but he, too, anticipates the time when he will have many

The Bible tells us that God will render to every man according to his deeds.

clients and he will be repaid for his toil. A great many medical students have a hard time trying to support themselves while they are at college. As soon as they get their diplomas and become doctors, though, they expect that the reaping time is near. That is what they have been working for.

Some harvests ripen almost immediately, but generally we find it true in the natural world that there is some delay before the seed comes to maturity. It is growing all the time, however. First the little green shoot breaks through the soil. Then we see the blade, the ear, and finally the full corn in the ear. The farmer is not disappointed that all his crops do not spring up in a night like mushrooms. He looks forward with patience, knowing that the reaping time will come in due season.

So it is with the harvest of our actions. Few people, if any, would indulge in sin unless they expected pleasure out of it. A drunkard does not drink for the mere sake of drinking, but in the hope of present enjoyment. A thief does not steal for the mere sake of stealing, but for the sake of gain. It is the same with the good man. He does not make sacrifices merely for the sake of sacrifice, but because in doing so he hopes and expects to do good and help others. All these things are means to an end; there is always expectation of a harvest.

The Certainty of the Reaping

The text wants us to look forward to the certainty of the reaping: *Whatever a man sows that shall he also reap* (Galatians 6:7).

We know what it is to have a failure of crops, but no such failure is possible in the spiritual world. In the physical world, wet soil may rot the seed, frost may nip the early buds, or the weather may prove too wet or too dry to bring the crops to maturity, but none of these things occur to prevent the harvest of our actions. The Bible tells us that God will render to every man according to his deeds:

> *But after thy hardness and impenitent heart*
> *treasures up unto thyself wrath against the*
> *day of wrath and revelation of the righteous*
> *judgment of God, who will render to everyone*

> *according to his deeds: to those who perse-*
> *vered in well doing, glory and honour and*
> *incorruption, to those who seek eternal life;*
> *but unto those that are contentious and do*
> *not obey the truth, but are persuaded by*
> *unrighteousness, indignation and wrath.*
> (Romans 2:5-8)

How careful we should be of our actions in all depart-
ments of our being – physical, moral, and intellectual!
The deeds we do, the words we speak, and the thoughts
we harbor are all recorded and will meet their just
reward, for God is no respecter of persons.

It must not be overlooked that the harvest comes
as a necessary consequence of the sowing. It has been
said that God is not a kind of moral tyrant, as He is
so often regarded. He does not
sit on a throne attaching penalties to particular actions as they
come up for judgment. He has
laid down certain laws, of which
the law of sowing and reaping

The harvest comes as a necessary consequence of the sowing.

is one, and punishment is the natural outcome of sin.
There is no escape. It must be accepted and dealt with.
Though others may have to reap *with* you, no one can
reap *for* you.

The text teaches further that the harvest is one of
two kinds. There are two, and only two, directions
in which the law leads: (1) sowing to the flesh, and a
harvest of corruption, or (2) sowing to the Spirit, and
a harvest of everlasting life.

Sowing to the Flesh

Sowing to the flesh does not mean to simply take proper care of the body. The body was made in the image of God, and the body of a believer is a temple of the Holy Spirit. Therefore, we can be sure that proper care of the body is well-pleasing to God. "Sowing to the flesh" refers rather to giving in to the lusts of the body, indulging it, providing gratification for its unlawful desires at the expense of the soul, and indulging the animal tendencies that are sinful in their excess. Sowing to the flesh is scattering the seeds of selfishness, which always yields a harvest of corruption.

While we were in the flesh, the affections of the sins which were by the law worked in our members to bring forth fruit unto death (Romans 7:5). What does Paul say the works of the flesh are? *Adultery, fornication, uncleanness, lasciviousness, idolatry, witchcraft, hatred, variance, emulations, wrath, strife, seditions, heresies, envyings, murders, drunkenness, revellings, and such like* (Galatians 5:19-21).

I was at the Paris exhibition in 1867,[3] and I noticed a little oil painting there, only about a foot square, and the face was the most hideous I have ever seen. On the paper attached to the painting were the words, "Sowing the tares," and the face looked more like a demon's than a man's. As he sowed these tares, up came serpents and reptiles that were crawling on his body. All around

---

3   The *Exposition Universelle* (International Exposition) of 1867 was the largest world's fair. Millions of people attended this fair that celebrated scientific and industrial achievements and contained more than fifty thousand exhibits.

were woods with wolves and other animals prowling in them. I have seen that picture many times since. The reaping time is coming. If you sow to the flesh, you must reap the flesh. If you sow to the wind, you must reap the whirlwind (Hosea 8:7).

It must not be thought, though, that indulgence in the more obvious sins is the only way of sowing to the flesh. Every desire and every action that does not have God as its end and object is seed sown to the flesh. If someone is sowing for a harvest of money or fame, he is sowing to the flesh and will reap corruption, just as certainly as the liar and the adulterer. No matter how polite, refined, and respectable the seed may be and no matter how closely it resembles the good seed, its true nature will come out and the contamination of corruption will be upon it.

How foolish are the strivings of so many people in view of this judgment! Many people will sacrifice time, health, and even character for money. What does he gain? Corruption – something that is not eternal and does not have the qualities of everlasting life. The apostle John said, *The world passes away and the lust thereof* (1 John 2:17), and Peter tells us, *All flesh is as grass, and all the glory of man as the flower of grass. The grass withers, and its flower falls away* (1 Peter 1:24). None of these fleshly things have their roots in the eternal. You might even outlive them in your own short life.

No Bridge Between

People make the mistake of sowing to the flesh while

thinking they will reap the harvest of the Spirit. On the other hand, they sow to the Spirit and are disappointed when they do not reap a worldly harvest.

A Sunday school teacher had been telling his class about the parable of the rich man and Lazarus. He asked, "Which would you rather be – the rich man or Lazarus?"

One boy answered, "I would rather be the rich man while I live and Lazarus when I die."

That cannot be. It is either flesh and corruption or Spirit and everlasting life. There is no bridge from one to the other.

Seed that is sown for a spiritual harvest has no tendency whatsoever to produce earthly well-being. Christ declared:

> *Blessed are those that mourn, for they shall be comforted. Blessed are the meek, for they shall inherit the earth. Blessed are those who hunger and thirst for righteousness, for they shall be satisfied. Blessed are the merciful, for they shall obtain mercy. Blessed are the pure in heart, for they shall see God.* (Matthew 5:4-8)

You can see the holy vision of the Almighty – fullness of righteousness and divine comfort. There is nothing earthly here. It is spiritual results for spiritual labor. It is not said that the pure in heart will be made rich, or that those who hunger and thirst after righteousness will be satisfied with bread (but rather, they will be filled with righteousness), or that those who mourn will rise in life and become famous. Each department has its own appropriate harvest reserved exclusively for its own method of sowing.

Everything reaps its own harvest; every act has its own reward. Before you covet the enjoyment that someone else possesses, you must first calculate the cost at which it was obtained. For instance, the Christian businessman complains that his honesty is a hindrance to his success – that the tide of money pours into the doors of his less honest neighbor, while he himself waits for hours without any sales. My brother, do you think that God is going to reward honor, integrity, and holiness with this world's rewards? Do you think that He will repay spiritual excellence with money and fame?

> Everything reaps its own harvest; every act has its own reward.

Consider the price that man has paid for his worldly success – perhaps mental shame and inward dishonor. His advertisements are all deceptive, his treatment of his employees tyrannical, and his cheap prices made possible by inferior material. If you sow that man's seed, you will reap that man's harvest. Money might come to you if you cheat, lie, and are dishonest in what you say, but if the price is too high, and I assure you that it is, let him have his harvest and you will have yours – a clear conscience, a pure mind, and righteousness within and without. Will you give that up for the worldly person's harvest?

Sowing to the Spirit

Sowing to the Spirit implies denying self, resisting evil, obeying the Spirit, walking in the Spirit, living in the Spirit, and being guided by the Spirit. We sow to the Spirit when we use our abilities and means to advance spiritual things. We sow to the Spirit when we support and encourage those who are extending the influence of the Spirit. We sow to the Spirit when we crucify the flesh and all its lusts, and when we yield ourselves to Him as we once yielded ourselves to the flesh. A Jewish rabbi once said, "There are in every person two impulses: good and evil. He who yields his evil impulses to God offers the best sacrifice."

The fruit of such sowing is *charity, joy, peace, tolerance, gentleness, goodness, faith, meekness, temperance: against such there is no law. For those that are of the Christ have crucified the flesh with its affections and lusts* (Galatians 5:22-24). In this world, the harvest is growth of character, deeper respect, and increasing usefulness to others; in the next world, the harvest is acceptance by God and everlasting life.

Among the last recorded words of [William] Lloyd Garrison in his public speeches in England were these: "I began my advocacy of the anti-slavery cause in the northern states of America in the midst of bricks and rotten eggs, and I ended it on the soil of South Carolina almost literally buried beneath the wreaths of flowers that were heaped upon me by her liberated bondmen."

A young man was employed by a large firm in New York City during the late Civil War to negotiate with a certain party for a load of damaged beans. The beans were purchased, delivered, and spread out upon the upper floor of the building occupied by the firm. Men were employed to turn them over and over and to sprinkle them with a solution of soda, so as to improve their appearance and render them more salable. A large load of good quality beans was then purchased. Some of the good beans were first put into barrels, then the barrels were nearly filled with the poor ones. After this, the good ones were again put on the top and the barrels were closed up.

The employer marked the barrels, "Beans – A1." The clerk saw and asked, "Do you think, sir, that it is right to mark those beans 'A1'?"

The employer retorted sharply, "Are you the head of the firm?"

The clerk said no more. The barreling continued. When all was ready, the beans (many hundreds of barrels) were put on the market for sale. Specimens of the best quality were shown in the office to buyers.

Later, a clever purchaser came in (no one is so sharp in business that he will not often meet his equal), examined the samples in the office, asked the price, and then wanted to see the stock in bulk. The clerk was ordered to go with the buyer to the upper loft and show him the stock. An open barrel was shown of apparently the same quality as that of the sample. The buyer then said to the clerk, "Young man, the samples of beans shown to me are of the first quality, and it is impossible to purchase beans anywhere in the market for the price at which you offer them; there is something wrong here.

Tell me, are these beans the same quality throughout the entire barrel as they appear on the top?"

The clerk now found himself in a difficult position. He thought, "Should I lie for my employer, as he undoubtedly wants me to, or should I tell the truth, no matter what the result may be?"

He decided for the truth and said, "No, sir. They are not."

"Then," said the customer, "I do not want them," and he left.

The clerk entered the office. The employer asked him, "Did you sell that man those beans?"

He said, "No, sir."

"Why not?"

"Well, sir, the man asked me if those beans were of the same quality throughout the entire barrel as they were on the top. I told him they were not. He then said, 'I do not want them,' and he left."

"Go to the cashier," said the employer, "and get your wages; we don't want you any longer." He received his pay and left the office, rejoicing that he had not lied for the purposes of assisting in dishonest greed and benefiting an unprincipled employer.

Three weeks after this, the firm sent for the young clerk and asked him to come back again and work for them. They offered him three hundred dollars more per year as a salary than they had ever before given him. Thus his honesty and truthfulness were rewarded. The firm knew and felt that the man was right, although apparently they had lost much money by his honesty. They wanted to have him again in their employment, because they knew that they could trust him and would never suffer through fraud and deception. They knew that their financial interests would be safe in his custody. They respected and honored that young man.

The Lesson of Patience

Let us learn the lesson of patience. *Behold, the husbandman waits for the precious fruit of the earth, waiting patiently until it receives the early and latter rain* (James 5:7). Delay does not necessarily mean denial. Too often one generation sows and another has to reap. God is *a jealous God, visiting the iniquity of the fathers upon the sons unto the third and fourth generation of those that hate me* (Deuteronomy 5:9).

Delay does not necessarily mean denial.

In the early years of Israel's existence as a separate people, God commanded them to give the land of Canaan rest every seven years:

> *Six years thou shalt sow thy land and shalt gather in its increase, but the seventh year thou shalt leave it free and release it, that the poor of thy people may eat, and what they leave the beasts of the field shall eat. In like manner thou shalt deal with thy vineyard and with thy oliveyard.* (Exodus 23:10-11)

From the time of the anointing of Saul to be king, this law was not observed. After 490 years, God gave the nation into captivity for seventy years. During this period, the land had seventy sabbath years of rest to compensate for the sabbath years of which it had been deprived. Those Israelites sowed the bitter seed of disobedience, and their descendants had to reap the harvest in exile and captivity.

A leading surgeon performed a critical operation in front of his class one day. The operation was successful, as far as his part was concerned. However, he turned to the class and said, "Six years ago a wise way of living might have prevented this disease. Two years ago, a safe and simple operation might have cured it. We have done our best today as the case now stands, but nature will have her word to say. She does not always repeal her death sentences." The next day the patient died, reaping the fruit of his excesses. Paul says, *Let us not be weary in well doing, for in due season we shall reap if we faint not* (Galatians 6:9).

In a chat with an interviewer, Thomas Edison quite unconsciously preached a most powerful sermon on perseverance and patience. He described his repeated efforts to make the phonograph reproduce the aspirated sound, and then he added, "From eighteen to twenty hours a day for the last seven months I have worked on the single word *specia*. I said into the phonograph, 'specia, specia, specia,' but the instrument responded, 'pecia, pecia, pecia.' It was enough to drive one insane! But I held firm, and I have succeeded."

An insurance case was brought to Daniel Webster when he was a young lawyer in Portsmouth, New Hampshire. Only a small amount of money was involved, and a twenty-dollar fee was all that was promised. Webster realized that to do his client full justice, he would need to travel to Boston in order to consult the law library. He would use all the money by going there, and he would receive no adequate compensation for his time there, but he determined to do his best, whatever it cost. So Webster went to Boston, looked up the law, and won the case.

Years later, Webster, who had meanwhile become famous, was passing through New York. An important insurance case was to be tried that day, and one of the lawyers had suddenly been taken ill. Money was no object, and Webster was begged to name his terms and conduct the case.

"I told them," said Mr. Webster, "that it was preposterous to expect me to prepare a legal argument with only a few hours' notice. They insisted, however, that I should look at the papers, and I finally consented to do so. It was my old twenty-dollar case all over again, and as I never forget anything, I had all the authorities at my fingertips. The court knew that I had no time to prepare, and they were astonished at the range of the arguments of my case. So you see, I was handsomely repaid both in fame and money for that journey to Boston. The moral is that good work is rewarded in the end."

Two men were digging for gold in California. They worked for a long while and got nothing. At last, one of them threw down his tools and said, "I will leave here before we starve," and he left. His comrade's patience was rewarded the next day when he found a nugget that supported him until he made a fortune.

> *Because the sentence against an evil work is*
> *not executed speedily, therefore the heart of*
> *the sons of men is fully set in them to do evil.*
> *Though a sinner does evil one hundred times*
> *and his judgment is prolonged, yet surely I*
> *know that it shall be well with those that fear*
> *God, who fear before his presence; but it shall*
> *never be well with the wicked, neither shall*
> *his days be prolonged, which are as a shadow,*
> *because he did not fear before the presence of*
> *God.* (Ecclesiastes 8:11-13)

The idea that something will never be brought to light because it is done in the dark is fatal. God says it will be brought to light. It is foolishness for someone who has covered his sins to think they will not be found out and that there will be no final judgment. Look at the sons of Jacob. They sold Joseph and deceived their father. Twenty long years rolled by, and their sin followed them way down to Egypt, for they said, *We are truly guilty concerning our brother* (Genesis 42:21). The reaping time had come at last for those ten boys who sold their brother.

I was once preaching in Chicago, and a woman who was nearly out of her mind came to me. There are

The idea that something will never be brought to light because it is done in the dark is fatal.

some people who mock at religious meetings and say that religion drives people insane. It is *sin* that drives people crazy. It is the lack of Christ that sinks people into despair.

This woman had a family of children. One of her neighbors had died, and her husband had brought home a little child. She said, "I don't want the child," but her husband said, "You must take it and look after it." She said she had enough to do with her own children, and she told her husband to take that child away – but he would not. She confessed that she tried to starve the child, but it lingered on. One night it cried all night. I suppose it wanted food. At last she took the clothes and threw them over the child and smothered it. No one saw her do it. No one knew anything about it. The child was buried. Years had passed away, but she said, "I hear the voice of that child day and night. It has driven me nearly insane." No one saw the act, but God had seen it, and this retribution followed it. You do not need to go to the Bible to find it out. History is full of these things.

Chapter 4

We Expect to Reap the Same Kind As We Sow

The earth brought forth green grass and herb yielding seed after its kind and the tree yielding fruit whose seed was in itself, according to its nature. (Genesis 1:12)

Do men gather grapes of thorns, or figs of thistles? (Matthew 7:16)

For if ye live according to the flesh, ye shall die; but if through the Spirit ye mortify the deeds of the body, ye shall live. (Romans 8:13)

If I told you that I planted ten acres of wheat last year and watermelons came up, or that I sowed cucumbers and gathered turnips, you wouldn't believe it. It is a fixed law that you reap the same kind of seed you sow. Plant wheat and you reap wheat. Plant an acorn and there comes up an oak tree. Plant a little elm and in time you have a big elm.

One day the master of Lukman, an Eastern writer of fables, said to him, "Go into that field and sow barley." Lukman sowed oats instead. At the time of harvest his master went to the field and saw the green oats springing up. He asked Lukman, "Did I not tell you to sow barley here? Why then have you sown oats?"

He answered, "I sowed oats in the hope that barley would grow up."

His master said, "What foolish idea is this? Have you ever heard anything like this?"

Lukman replied, "You yourself are constantly sowing the seeds of evil in the field of the world, and yet expect to reap the fruits of virtue in the resurrection day. Therefore, I thought also that I might get barley by sowing oats." The master was ashamed at the reply and set Lukman free.

Like produces like in vegetation, and like produces like in labor. If a man has learned the trade of a carpenter, he does not expect to excel as a watchmaker. If he has toiled hard to acquire a knowledge of the law, he does not expect to practice medicine for a livelihood. People expect to reap in the same line as they have learned.

This law is just as true in God's kingdom as in man's kingdom. It is just as true in the spiritual world as in the natural world. If I sow tares, I am going to reap tares. If I sow a lie, I am going to reap lies. If I sow adultery, I am going to reap adulterers. If I sow whisky, I am going to reap drunkards. You cannot blot this law out, for it is always in force. No other truth in the Bible is more firm.

Suppose that a neighbor whom I don't want to see

comes to my house, and I tell my son to tell him that I am out of town. My son goes to the door and lies to my neighbor. It will not be six months before my son will lie to me. I will reap that lie.

A man asked me some time ago, "Why is it that we cannot get honest clerks nowadays?"

I replied, "I don't know, but maybe I can come up with a reason. When merchants teach clerks to say that goods are all wool when they are half cotton, or when they teach their salespeople to tell half-truths or exaggerate in order to make a sale, you will not have honest clerks."

> As long as merchants teach their clerks to lie and to misrepresent, they will have dishonest clerks.

As long as merchants teach their clerks to lie and to misrepresent, they will have dishonest clerks. Dishonest merchants make dishonest clerks. I am not talking fiction – I am talking truth. It is not an imaginative poem, but it is sincere prose that a person must reap the same kind of seed that he sows.

This is a tremendous argument against selling alcohol. Even if we leave out the abstinence and religious aspects of the question of alcohol, no one on earth can afford to sell strong drink. If I sell alcohol to your son and make a drunkard of him, someone may sell alcohol to my son and make a drunkard of him. Everyone who sells alcohol has a drunken son or a drunken brother or some drunken relative. Where are the sons of alcohol dealers? To whom are their daughters married? Look around and see if you can find a man who has been in that business twenty years who doesn't have a skeleton in his own family.

I threw that challenge down once, and a man said to me the next day, "I wasn't at your meeting last night, but I understand you made the astounding statement that no man had been in the alcohol business twenty years who didn't have the curse in his own family."

"Yes," I said, "I did."

"It isn't true," he said, "and I want you to take it back. My father sold alcohol, and I sell alcohol, and the curse has never come into my father's family or into mine."

I said, "What! Two generations selling that infernal stuff, and the curse has never come into the family? I will investigate it, and if I find I am wrong, I will make the retraction just as publicly as I did the statement."

There were two prominent citizens of the town in the room, and I noticed a strange expression on their faces as the man was talking. After he left, one of the men said, "Do you know, Mr. Moody, that man's own brother was a drunkard and committed suicide a few weeks ago? He left a widow with seven children. They are under his roof now! He was a terrible drunkard himself until the shock of his brother's suicide cured him."

I don't know how you can account for this unless he thought his brother wasn't a relative. Perhaps he was sort of like Cain, asking, *Am I my brother's keeper?* (Genesis 4:9).

When I was a pastor of a church in Chicago, we were trying to reach the working men for Christ. They used to say to me, "Come down to the factory at dinnertime and we will give you a chance to speak."

I would ask them, "Why won't you come to the church?"

"Oh," they would say, "you have it all your own way there, and we can't answer back; but come to the factory and we will pose a few questions to you."

So I went down, and they made it pretty hot for me at times. One of the favorite biblical characters that they brought up was Jacob. Many times I have had men say, "You think Jacob was a saint, don't you? He was a big rascal." Many have said they thought Jacob wasn't as good as Esau. Notice what you read in the Bible: *The Lord also has a controversy with Judah to visit Jacob according to his ways; according to his doings will he recompense him* (Hosea 12:2). This law of retribution runs through his life. Although he was a friend of God, a relative of Abraham, and was third in the line of the covenant, God made Jacob reap the same kind of seed he sowed. Someone has said that Jacob's problems were uniformly calculated to bring back to his remembrance the picture as well as the punishment of his faults.

When Isaac in his old age wanted some venison and sent Esau out to get it, Jacob slipped out and took a goat from his father's flock, and Rebekah, his mother, cooked it. He brought it to his old, blind father and said he was Esau. The old man recognized Jacob's voice, but Jacob had very cunningly put the skin of the goat on his hands and neck so that the old man felt him and said, *The voice is Jacob's voice, but the hands are the hands of Esau* (Genesis 27:22).

He got his brother's birthright blessing by this lie, but he paid ten thousand times more for it than it was worth. "He who steals my purse steals trash." A man who steals my wallet suffers more than I do. When Jacob had grown to be an old man, he lived in continual suspicion that his sons were deceiving him. The sin of deceiving his own father bore fruit.

Jacob was the big loser in this transaction. When Esau returned, Jacob had to flee for his life. Then God met him at Bethel:

> *And, behold, the Lord stood above it and said, I AM the God of Abraham, thy father, and the God of Isaac; the land upon which thou dost lie, to thee will I give it and to thy seed; and thy seed shall be as the dust of the earth, and thou shalt multiply to the west and to the east and to the Aquilon and to the Negev; and in thee and in thy seed shall all the families of the earth be blessed. And, behold, I am with thee and will keep thee in all places where thou goest and will bring thee again into this land; for I will not leave thee until I have done that which I have spoken to thee of.* (Genesis 28:13-15)

People will read that far in the life of Jacob and say, "I don't want anything more to do with a God who will deal in grace with a man who had done so mean a thing." My friend, hold on. Follow him to Padanaram. He was there twenty years, and during that time his wages were changed ten times. He worked seven years for the lovely Rachel, and then was tricked into marrying Rachel's sister, Leah. Jacob had obtained the blessing of the firstborn son by deception, but Laban sarcastically reminded him, *It must not be so done in our country to give the younger before the firstborn* (Genesis 29:26). Jacob learned that Laban could drive as sharp a bargain as he could.

Wherever you find a sharp, shrewd man, you will always find that he attracts the same kind of people around him, and that he who cheats will himself be cheated. "Birds of a feather flock together." Blasphemers get together, and sharp, shrewd people get together. Jacob found in Laban just such a man as himself. It was "diamond cut diamond."

> A man who steals my wallet suffers more than I do.

Look a little further. Jacob had twelve sons, but he loved Joseph and Benjamin more than the others because they were the sons of his beloved Rachel. He was partial to Joseph and had a coat of many colors made for him. Favoritism will raise the old Adam in any family.

One morning, Joseph, in the innocence of his heart, told of a dream he had in which his father and all his brothers had bowed down to him. Then his brothers began to plan to get him out of the way, and when his father sent him to find them when they were tending the flocks, they said, *Let us slay him and cast him into a cistern, and we will say, Some evil beast has devoured him* (Genesis 37:20).

They later sold him, took his coat of many colors, and dipped it in the blood of a goat. They took that coat to their father and said, *We have found this, recognize now whether it is thy son's coat or not* (Genesis 37:32). He knew it was Joseph's coat, and he said, *It is my son's coat; an evil beast has devoured him* (Genesis 37:33).

Notice that Jacob deceived his father with the skin of a goat, and his sons deceived him with the blood of a goat. Jacob lied to his father, and his sons lied to him. The lie came home. Every lie is bound to come back to you. You cannot dig a grave so deep that the lie will not have a resurrection.

Be sure your sin will catch up with you (Numbers 32:23). You may think you are very clever and wise and can plan and cover up, but it is the decree of high heaven that no sin will be covered; God will uncover it. You can be sure that your sin will find you out. You cannot deceive the Almighty. Jacob found that out. He had to reap what he sowed.

Look at David once again. A man said to me some years ago, "Don't you think David fell as low as Saul?" Yes, he fell lower, because God had lifted him higher. The difference is that when Saul fell, there was no sign of repentance, but when David fell, a cry went up from his broken heart and there was true repentance. No one in all of Scripture rose so high and fell so low as David. God took him from the sheepfold and placed him on the throne. He gave him riches and lands in abundance. He was on a pinnacle of glory and was loved and honored among men. But one day, you remember, David was walking upon the roof of the king's house when he saw

You cannot deceive the Almighty.

Bathsheba and lusted after her, and he committed the awful sin of adultery. Then, to cover up that sin, he got Bathsheba's husband drunk and had him murdered. The Lord God declared: *I will raise up evil against thee out of thy own house* (2 Samuel 12:11), and *the sword shall never depart from thy house* (2 Samuel 12:10).

David's son Amnon then committed adultery with David's own daughter. David's son Absalom made a feast for Amnon and had him murdered. Not long after that, Absalom came with an army to drive his own father, David, from the throne, and he publicly committed adultery with David's concubines on the roof of the king's house. If God had not been overruling, Absalom would have killed his father.

David sowed adultery and reaped it in his own family. He sowed murder and reaped it in his own family. I believe that what brought the bitter cry from that father's heart – *O my son Absalom, my son, my son Absalom! I would rather have died instead of thee, O Absalom, my son, my son!* (2 Samuel 18:33) – was the fact that these were the wages of his own sin. From the time David fell into that sin with Uriah's wife until he went down to his grave, it was one billow after another rolling over him.

If God did not spare David, do you think He will spare us if we fall into sin and do not confess and turn from our sins? If ever anyone had an opportunity to cover his sins, David did. No judge or jury dared to pronounce judgment against him. The deed was done in the dark, but his sin found him out. Nathan was sent across his path, and, young man, Nathan will appear to you some day. Some messenger will smite you in the way if you do not repent and turn from your sins. My friend, why not call on God now as David did when he came to himself? Make the same prayer. How thankful we should be that we have that prayer! Why not get on your knees now and pray?

David's Prayer for Forgiveness

Have mercy upon me, O God, according to thy mercy; according unto the multitude of thy compassion eradicate my rebellion. Wash me thoroughly from my iniquity and cleanse me from my sin. For I acknowledge my rebellion; and my sin is ever before me. Against thee, against thee only, have I sinned and done this evil in thy sight that thou be declared just in thy word and pure in thy judgment. Behold, the pain of my iniquity has caused me to writhe; my mother conceived me so that sin might be removed from me.

Behold, thou dost desire truth in the inward parts, and in the secret things thou hast made me to know wisdom. Remove the sin in me with hyssop, and I shall be clean; wash me, and I shall be whiter than snow. Make me to hear joy and gladness that the bones which thou hast broken may rejoice. Hide thy face from my sins and eradicate all my iniquities.

*Create in me a clean heart, O God, and
renew a right spirit within me. Cast me not
away from thy presence and take not thy Holy
Spirit from me. Restore unto me the joy of thy
saving health, and thy spirit of liberty shall
uphold me. Then I will teach transgressors
thy ways, and sinners shall be converted unto
thee.*

*Deliver me from bloodguiltiness, O God, thou
God of my salvation, and my tongue shall
sing aloud of thy righteousness. O Lord, open
my lips; and my mouth shall show forth thy
praise. For thou dost not desire sacrifice or
else would I give it; thou dost not delight in
burnt offering. The sacrifices of God are a
broken spirit: a broken and a contrite heart,
O God, thou wilt not despise.*

*Do good in thy good pleasure unto Zion; build
thou the walls of Jerusalem. Then thou shalt
be pleased with the sacrifices of righteousness,
the burnt offering, the offering that has been
totally consumed by the fire; then shall they
offer bullocks upon thine altar.* (Psalm 51)

Examples from History

You might claim that you don't believe in the Bible.
Then look at history and see if this law of reaping what
you sow is not true. Maxentius built a false bridge to

drown Constantine, but was drowned himself. Bajazet was carried about by Tamerlane in an iron cage that he intended for Tamerlane. Maximinus put out the eyes of thousands of Christians, but soon after, a fearful disease of the eyes broke out among his people, of which he himself died in great agony. Valens caused about eighty Christians to be sent to sea in a ship and burned alive; he was defeated by the Goths and fled to a cottage where he was burned alive.

Alexander VI was poisoned by wine he had prepared for another. Henry III of France was stabbed in the same chamber where he had helped to contrive the cruel massacre of French Protestants. Marie Antoinette, riding to Notre Dame Cathedral for her wedding, ordered the soldiers to command all beggars, cripples, and raggedly clothed people to leave the line of the procession. She could not endure the sight of these miserable ones. Soon after, bound in the executioner's cart, she was riding toward the place of execution amid crowds who gazed on her with hearts as cold as ice and hard as granite. When Foullon was asked how the starving populace was to live, he said, "Let them eat grass." Afterward, the mob, maddened with rage, caught him on the streets of Paris, hung him, stuck his head upon a pike, and filled his mouth with grass.

Chapter 5

A Man Reaps More than He Sows

But some fell into good ground and brought forth fruit: one a hundredfold and another sixtyfold and another thirtyfold. (Matthew 13:8)

The Spaniards have this proverb: "Sow a thought and reap an act. Sow an act and reap a habit. Sow a habit and reap a character. Sow a character and reap a destiny." If I sow a bushel, I expect to reap ten or twenty bushels. I can sow in one day what will take ten men to reap. I have heard of a certain kind of bean that reproduces itself a thousandfold. One thistledown that blew from the deck of a vessel is said to have covered the entire surface of a South Sea island with thistles. An oak tree springs from an acorn, and the mighty Mississippi River begins from a little spring.

One glass of whisky may lead to a drunkard's death. One lie may ruin a man's career. One error in youth may follow a person all through life. Someone has said that many Christians spend half their time trying to keep down the sprouts of seed that was sown in their young days. Unless it is held in check, the desire to have a drink will become a consuming thirst; the desire to play a game of cards will become an irresistible gambler's passion.

Abraham gave up his only son at God's command, and as the fruit of that act of obedience, God gave him descendants as numerous as the stars of the heavens and as the sands upon the seashore.

Jacob told one lie, and his ten sons came back with his lie multiplied tenfold. For twenty years Jacob mourned for Joseph, supposing that he was dead. I have no doubt that night after night he wept for Joseph, and in his dreams he saw the boy torn to pieces and heard his cries for help. It took him a long time to reap the harvest.

Israel murmured against God because of the report of the land of Canaan brought back by the spies. Did they not have to reap a multiplied harvest as a result? Listen to what the Lord says to them: *After the number of the days in which ye spied out the land, even forty days, each day for a year, ye shall bear your iniquities forty years, and ye shall know my reason for annulling my promise* (Numbers 14:34).

When I made the remark in a meeting once that a man had to reap more than he sowed, a man in front of me dropped his head and sobbed aloud. After the meeting, a friend stepped up to him and asked, "What is your trouble?"

He pointed to me and said, "Every word that man has been saying is true. Four years ago I was the confidential clerk of a firm in this city. I have reason to believe that if I had continued as I began, I would still be in the firm now. But one night in a saloon, under the influence of alcohol, I committed a crime, and I was sent to the penitentiary, where I repented in sackcloth and ashes. Today I came back for the first time. I went to my old place of employment, and they ordered me out. I went to other businesses I was acquainted with, and I received the same treatment. I met men on the street whom I once knew who had held inferior positions to me, and I lifted my hat, but no one returned the bow." The man wrung his hands in agony and said, "It is all true. It takes a longer time to reap than to sow."

> It takes a long time to build up a character, but you can destroy it in a single hour.

Do you not believe it? Ask your neighbor who has drunk up his character, his reputation, and his home, and has brought trouble on his family. It takes a long time to build up a character, but you can destroy it in a single hour.

A man died in the Columbus penitentiary some years ago who had spent over thirty years in his cell. He had been one of the millionaires of Ohio. Fifty years ago, when they were trying to build a road from Chicago to New York, they wanted to lay the line through his farm near Cleveland. He did not want his farm divided by the railroad, so the case went to court, where commissioners were appointed to pay the damages and to allow the road to be built.

One dark night after the tracks were laid, a train was thrown off the track and several people were killed. This man was suspected. He was tried, found guilty, and was sent to the penitentiary for life. The farm was soon cut up into city lots, and the man became a millionaire – but he got no benefit from it. It may not have taken him more than an hour to lay the obstruction on the railroad tracks, but he spent more than thirty years reaping the result of that one act! Thankfully, the chaplain told me that before this man died, he became a child of God. Yet, he had to live with the consequences of his actions even after giving his life to Christ.

In the history of France, we read that a certain king wanted a new instrument with which to torture his prisoners. One of his favorite advisors suggested that he should build a cage that was not long enough to lie down in and not high enough to stand up in. The king accepted the suggestion, but the first one put into the cage was the very man who suggested it, and he was kept in it for fourteen years. It did not take him more than a few minutes to suggest that cruel device, but he was fourteen long years reaping the fruit of what he had sown.

If a man could do his reaping alone, it would not be so hard, but it is terrible when he has to make his godly father, and his mother who loves him, or his wife and family reap along with him. Does not the drunkard make his wife and children reap a bitter harvest? Does not the gambler make his relatives reap? Does not the prostitute make her parents reap agony and shame? What a bitter enemy sin is! May God help each one of us turn from it at once!

Whenever I hear a young man talking in a thoughtless way about sowing his wild oats, I don't laugh. I feel more like crying, because I know he is going to make his gray-haired mother reap in tears. He is going to make his wife reap in shame. He is going to make his old father and his innocent children reap with him. Only ten or fifteen or twenty years will pass before he will have to reap his wild oats; no one has ever sowed them without having to reap them. *They have sown the wind, and they shall reap the whirlwind* (Hosea 8:7).

We cannot control our influence. If I plant thistles in my field, the wind will take the thistledown when it is ready and will blow it away beyond the fence, and my neighbors will have to reap with me. In the same way, my example may be copied by my children or my neighbors, and my actions may be reproduced indefinitely through them, whether for good or evil. How many have gone to ruin because of the sins of such men as Jacob and David and Lot!

Nothing but Leaves

Nothing but leaves! The Spirit grieves
    O'er years of wasted life;
O'er sins indulged while conscience slept,
O'er vows and promises unkept,
    And reap, from years of strife –
Nothing but leaves! Nothing but leaves!

Nothing but leaves! No gathered sheaves
　　Of life's fair ripening grain:
We sow our seeds; lo! tares and weeds,
Words, idle words, for earnest deeds –
　　Then reap, with toil and pain,
Nothing but leaves! Nothing but leaves!

Nothing but leaves! Sad memory weaves
　　No veil to hide the past;
And as we trace our weary way,
And count each lost and misspent day,
　　We sadly find at last –
Nothing but leaves! Nothing but leaves!

Ah, who shall thus the Master meet,
　　And bring but withered leaves?
Ah, who shall, at the Savior's feet,
Before the awful judgment seat,
　　Lay down, for golden sheaves,
Nothing but leaves! Nothing but leaves!
　　– Lucy Evilena Akerman

*When he came to her, he found nothing but
leaves* (Mark 11:13).

Chapter 6

Ignorance of the Seed Makes No Difference

*Marvel not at this, for an hour shall come
when all that are in the graves shall hear his
voice, and those that have done good shall
come forth unto the resurrection of life; but
those that have done evil, unto the resurrection of judgment.* (John 5:28-29)

Notice that ignorance of the kind of seed makes
no difference. If I think I am sowing good seed
and it happens to be bad, I will have a bad harvest;
therefore, I need to take note of what kind of seed I
am sowing.

Suppose I meet a man who is sowing seed, and I
say to him, "Hello, stranger. What are you sowing?"

"Seed," he says.

"What kind of seed?"

"I don't know."

"Don't you know what will grow?"

"No, I can't tell, but it is seed; that is all I need to know, and I am sowing it."

You would say that he was a first-class lunatic, wouldn't you? But he wouldn't be half as crazy as the man who goes on sowing for time and eternity and never asks himself what he is sowing or what the harvest will be.

Father, what seed are you sowing in your family? Are you setting your children a good or a bad example? Do you spend your time at the saloon or the club until you have become almost a stranger to them, or are you training them for God and righteousness?

Father, what seed are you sowing in your family?

A man once said that he would not talk to his son about Christianity, but that the boy should make his own decision when he grew up, without being influenced by him. Well, the boy broke his arm, and as the doctor was setting it, the boy cursed and swore the whole time.

"Ah," said the doctor to the father, "you were afraid to influence the boy in the right way, but the devil had no such prejudice. He has led your son the other way." How sad the idea that a father is to let his children run wild! Nature alone doesn't bring forth anything but weeds.

One of Samuel Taylor Coleridge's friends once objected to prejudicing the minds of the young by selecting the things they should be taught. The philosopher-poet invited him to take a look at his garden, and he took him to where an abundant growth of ugly and nonfragrant weeds spread themselves over beds and walks alike.

"You don't call that a garden!" said his friend.

"What!" said Coleridge. "Would you have me prejudice the ground in favor of roses and lilies?"

Have you never noticed the same thing about the mind and the heart? Let a child be idle, and Satan will soon lead him into mischief. He must be looked after. Those things that will help to develop character must be selected for him, and hurtful things must be kept out, just as diligently as the farmer cultivates the useful products of the soil but wages continual war on weeds and all unwholesome growths.

A murderer was to suffer the penalty of his crime. Speaking of his reckless career, he said, "How could it be otherwise, when I had such bad training? I was taught these things from my youth. When I was only four years old, my mother poured whisky down my throat to see how I would act." On the morning of his execution, the wretched mother said good-bye to the son whom her influence had helped lead to that shameful end.

A father started for his office early one morning after a light snowfall. He turned and saw his two-year-old boy trying to put his tiny feet in his own big footprints. The little fellow shouted, "Go on. I'se comin', Papa. I'se comin' right in your tracks!" He caught the boy in his arms, carried him to his mother, and started again for his office.

His habit had been to stop at a saloon on the way to work for a glass of liquor. As he stood upon the threshold of the saloon that morning, he seemed to hear a sweet voice say, "Go on. I'se comin', Papa. I'se comin' right in your tracks." He stopped, hesitated, and looked the future squarely in the face. "I cannot afford to make any tracks I would be ashamed or sorry to have my boy walk in," he said decidedly, and he turned away.

Father, mother, neighbor – are your tracks true? Are they straight? Can you turn to anyone walking behind you and say, "Follow me as I follow Christ"? Are you leading the little ones safely to the Good Shepherd? *Be ye imitators of me, even as I also am of Christ* (1 Corinthians 11:1).

The best time to sow the good seed is before Satan has scattered the tares. God has given numerous warnings and instructions to do so. *Seek ye first the kingdom of God and his righteousness* (Matthew 6:33). *Train up a child in the way he should go* (Proverbs 22:6). *Provoke not your children to wrath, but bring them up in the discipline and admonition of the Lord* (Ephesians 6:4). If a farmer neglects to plant in the springtime, he can never recover the lost opportunity, and neither can you if you neglect your opportunity. Youth is a seedtime, and if it is allowed to pass without good seed being sown, weeds will spring up and choke the soil. It will take bitter toil to uproot them.

An old theologian said that when a good farmer sees a weed in his field, he has it pulled up. If it is pulled up early enough, the bald patch is soon filled in and the crop waves over the whole field; but if it allowed to run too late, the bald patch remains. It would have been better if the weed had never been allowed to get root.

Young man, are you letting some secret sin get the mastery over you, binding you hand and foot? It is growing. Every sin grows. When I was speaking to five thousand children in Glasgow some years ago, I took a spool of thread and said to one of the largest boys, "Do you believe I can bind you with that thread?"

He laughed at the idea. I wound the thread around him a few times, and he broke it with a single jerk. Then I wound the thread around and around and around, and I said, "Now get free if you can." He couldn't move hand or foot. If you are slave to some sinful habit, you must either slay that habit or it will slay you.

My friend, what kind of seed are you sowing? Think about how you have lived for the past year. Have you been living a double life? Have you been making a profession of being a Christian without possessing what you profess? If there is anything you detest about how you are living, it is hypocrisy. Do you tell me God doesn't detest it also? If it is your right eye that causes you to sin, make up your mind that you will pluck it out. If it is your right hand or your right foot that causes you to stumble, cut it off (Matthew 5:29-30). Whatever the sin, make up your mind that you will gain the victory over it without further delay.

What kind of seed are you sowing, my friend – good seed or bad seed? There will be a harvest, and you are bound to reap, whether you want to or not. Tell me, how do you spend your spare time? Do you spend it telling sinful stories, polluting the minds of others while your own mind is also polluted? Do you read any literature that makes your thoughts impure?

How do you spend the Lord's Day? Do you spend it boating, fishing, hunting, or on trips? Do you think ministers are old-fashioned – that the Bible belongs to the Dark Ages?

Tell me how you treat your parents, and I will tell you how your children will treat you. A man was making preparations to send his old father to the poorhouse, when his little child came up and said to him, "Papa, when you are old will I have to take you to the poorhouse?"

Do you ever write home to your parents? They clothed you and educated you, and now do you spend your nights gambling? You tell your godless friends that your father crammed Christianity down your throat when you were a boy. I have great contempt for a man who says that of his father or mother. They may have made a mistake, but it was a mistake of the head, not of the heart.

If a message was sent to them that you were down with smallpox, they would immediately come to see you. They would willingly take the disease into their own bodies and die for you. If you scoff and sneer at your father and mother, you will have a hard harvest; you will reap in agony. It is only a question of time. There is a saying: "The mills of God grind slowly, but they grind exceeding small." The Lord Jesus said, *With the measure ye measure by, ye shall be measured by others* (Mark 4:24).

When I was last in London, a man told me that England had the advantage over America in one respect. I asked how. He said, "We have more respect for our laws in England than you do in America. You don't hang half your murderers, but all our murderers are hanged if they can be proved guilty."

I said, "Neither country hangs its worst murderers. If my son wants to murder me, I would rather have him kill me outright than to take five years to do it. The worst sort of a murderer is a young man who goes home late night after night, and when his mother reproves him of it, he curses her gray hairs and kills her by inches."

That is being done all over the country. You may not be guilty of a sin as black and as foul as this, but I tell you that every sin grows, and if you have sin in your heart, you cannot tell where it will land you. Nothing separates a son from his mother or a man from his wife like sin. The grace of God binds people together, but sin tears them apart and separates them.

> If you think you can give a loose rein to your passions and lusts and yet have eternal life, you are being deceived.

My friend, what kind of seed are you sowing? What will the harvest be? Will it be a sad and dreadful harvest, or are you going to have a joyful harvest? If you think that wheat will come up when you have sown tares, you are greatly mistaken. If you think you can give a loose rein to your passions and lusts and yet have eternal life, you are being deceived. God says, *He that sows to his flesh shall of the flesh reap corruption, but he that sows in the Spirit shall of the Spirit reap eternal life* (Galatians 6:8).

Choose Carefully

I beg you to carefully choose your path. The farmer is careful in the choice of seed. He does not want bad seed or inferior seed because he knows that such will give a poor crop. He looks for the best seed he can buy. If you choose to sow to the flesh, you will have a corrupted harvest. If you commit a sinful deed, it may land you in a dishonored grave.

Choice is a serious thing. You can make this moment a turning point in your life. Once during the conquest of Peru, Pizarro's followers threatened to desert him. They gathered on the shore to embark for home. Drawing his sword, he traced a line with it in the sand from east to west. Then turning toward the south, he said, "Friends and comrades, on that side are toil, hunger, nakedness, the drenching storm, and death. On this side are ease and pleasure. There lies Peru with all its riches; here lies Panama and its poverty. Let each man choose as becomes a brave Castilian. For my part, I go south." So saying, he stepped across the line, and one after another, his comrades followed him – and the destiny of South America was decided.

Napoleon was once offered a position as an officer in the Turkish artillery. He declined it, but if he had chosen to accept it, the history of Europe would have been different.

Your eternity depends upon your choice in spiritual things. On the one side there is Christ; on the other side is the world. You must choose between the two. Do not desire to grow both wheat and tares. Oh, choose

Christ! Let there be no halfheartedness. Give Him your whole heart. He died to redeem you from the curse of sin, and He lives to save you from the power of sin.

No one can serve two masters (Matthew 6:24). You cannot belong to two kingdoms at once. Lord Brougham grew to be so fond of Cannes, France, that he wanted to be naturalized as a Frenchman, but found it was impossible to be both a nobleman of England and a citizen of a French town; he had to renounce the one to become the other.

Now this is where the will comes in. It is easy to follow other people's leads and to swim with the tide, but it requires character and moral backbone to stand against the current of popular opinion and practice. During the late war, a deserter came into the Union lines in Pittsburgh. He was asked, "What did you go into secession for?"

His answer was, "Because they all did."

That reason will account for many people's actions. He will act according to the saying, "While you are in Rome, do as the Romans do," neglecting to investigate and determine whether or not the Romans do right. If they do wrong, you should stand against a whole nation, if need be, like Daniel did in Babylon.

Almighty God set two sides before the children of Israel, and I set them before you now. As you choose, remember that your eternity is in the balance.

> *See, I have set before thee this day life and good, and death and evil; for I command thee this day to love the Lord thy God, to walk in*

his ways, and to keep his commandments and his statutes and his rights, that thou may live and be multiplied; and may the Lord thy God bless thee in the land into which thou dost enter to inherit it.

But if thine heart turns away so that thou wilt not hear, but shalt be drawn away and worship other gods and serve them, I declare unto you this day that ye shall surely perish and that ye shall not prolong your days upon the land, to go unto which thou passest the Jordan to inherit it.

I call the heavens and the earth to witness today against you that I have set before you life and death, blessing and cursing; therefore, choose life that both thou and thy seed may live, that thou may love the Lord thy God and that thou may hear his voice and that thou may cleave unto him; for he is thy life and the length of thy days. (Deuteronomy 30:15-20)

Chapter 7

Forgiveness and Retribution

Thou renderest to every man according to his work. (Psalm 62:12)

We must all appear before the judgment seat of Christ that each one may receive according to that which they have done in the body, good or evil. (2 Corinthians 5:10)

I can imagine someone saying, "I attend church, and have heard that if we confess our sin, God will forgive us; now I hear that I must reap the same kind of seed that I have sown. How can I reconcile the doctrine of forgiveness with the doctrine of retribution? The Bible says, *All we like sheep have become lost; we have turned each one to his own way; and the LORD transposed in him the iniquity of us all* (Isaiah 53:6), yet you say that I must reap what I have sown."

Suppose I send my hired man to sow wheat, and when it grows up, there are thistles mixed with the wheat. There wasn't a thistle in my field a year ago, so I ask my hired man, "Do you know anything about the thistles in the field?"

He says, "Yes, I do. You sent me to sow that wheat, and I was angry and mixed some thistles with the wheat; but you promised me that if I ever did wrong and confessed it, you would forgive me. Now I hold you to that promise and expect you to forgive me."

"Yes," I say, "you are quite right. I forgive you for sowing the thistles, but I will tell you what you must do – you must reap the thistles along with the wheat when harvest time comes."

Many Christians are reaping thistles with their wheat. You might have sowed thistles with the wheat twenty years ago, and are reaping them now. Perhaps it was an obscene story, the memory of which keeps coming back to distress you, even at the most solemn moments. Maybe it was some hasty word or deed that you forgot about until now.

I heard John B. Gough say that he would rather cut off his hand than have committed a certain sin. He didn't say what it was, but I have always supposed it was the way he treated his mother. He was a wretched, habitual drunkard in the gutter when his mother died; the poor woman couldn't stand it and died of a broken heart. God had forgiven him, but he never forgave himself. A great many people have done things that they will never forgive themselves for to their dying day.

"At this moment," said one, "from many prostitutes' dishonored graves there arises a mute appeal for righteous retribution. From many drunkards' miserable homes, from heartbroken wives, from starving children, there rings up a terrible appeal into the ears of God."

I believe that God forgives sin fully and freely for Christ's sake, but He allows certain penalties to remain. If a man has wasted years in riotous living, he can never hope to live them over again. If he has violated his conscience, the scars will remain throughout his life. If he has stained his reputation, the effect of it can never be washed away. If he shatters his body through indulgence and wickedness, he must suffer until death. As the preacher T. De Witt Talmage said, "The grace of God gives a new heart, but not a new body."

> I believe that God forgives sin fully and freely for Christ's sake, but He allows certain penalties to remain.

"John," said a father to his son, "I would like you to get me the hammer."

"Yes, sir."

"Now get me a nail and a piece of pine board."

"Here they are, sir."

"Will you drive the nail into the board?" It was done. "Please pull it out again."

"That's easy, sir."

"Now, John," said the father as his voice dropped to a lower key, "pull out the nail hole."

Every wrong act leaves a scar. Even if the board is a living tree, the scar remains. There is plentiful redemption for our worst sins. My sin may become white as snow and pass away altogether, insofar as it has power to disturb or sadden my relationship with God, yet our least sins leave their traces and consequences in our lives, in our characters, in our memories, in our consciences, sometimes in our weakness, often in our worldly position, in our reputation, in our success, in our health, and in a thousand other ways. God will not put out His little finger to remove these, but He lets them stop.

Let no one think that the gospel that proclaims forgiveness can be lessened into a mere proclamation of impunity. This cannot be so. It was to Christians that Paul said, *Do not deceive yourselves; God is not mocked: for whatever a man sows that shall he also reap* (Galatians 6:7). God loves us too much not to punish His children when they sin, and He loves us too much to annihilate (if it were possible) the secondary consequences of our transgressions. The two sides of the truth must be recognized – that the deeper and (as we call them) the primary penalties of our evil, which are separation from God and the painful consciousness of guilt, are swept away, while other results are allowed to remain, which, being allowed, may be blessed and beneficial for those who have sinned.

MacLaren says:

> If you waste your youth, no repentance
> will send the shadow back upon the dial,
> or recover the ground lost by idleness, or
> restore the constitution shattered by dis-
> sipation, or give back the resources wasted
> upon vice, or bring back the fleeting oppor-
> tunities. . . . The wounds can all be healed

indeed, for the Good Physician, blessed be
His name, has lancets and bandages, and
balm and anodynes for the deadliest, but
scars remain even when the gash is closed.[4]

God forgave Moses and Aaron for their sins, but both
suffered the penalty. Neither one was permitted to
enter the promised land. Jacob became a prince of
God at the ford of Jabbok, but to
the end of his days he carried in
his body the mark of the struggle
(Genesis 32:28-31). Paul's thorn
in the flesh was not removed,
even after the most earnest and
repeated prayer. It lost its sting,
however, and became a means
of grace (2 Corinthians 12:7-9).

> **If the earthly
> consequences were
> completely removed,
> we would be likely to
> fall back again into sin.**

Perhaps that is one reason why God does not remove
these penalties of sin. He may intend them to be used
as tokens of His chastening. *The Lord chastens whom he
loves* (Proverbs 3:12). If the earthly consequences were
completely removed, we would be likely to fall back
again into sin. The penalty is a continual reminder of
our weakness and of the need of caution and dependence upon God.

One night in Chicago at the close of a meeting in
the YMCA rooms, a young man jumped to his feet and
said, "Mr. Moody, would you let me speak a few words?"

"Certainly," I said.

---

4   This quote is from Alexander Maclaren (1826-1910), an English
     non-conformist preacher, from his remarks on Psalm 99:8.

Then for about five minutes he pleaded with those men there to break from sin. He said: "If you have anyone who takes any interest in your spiritual welfare, treat them kindly, for they are the best friends you have. I was an only child, and my mother and father took great interest in me. Every morning at the family altar, my father used to pray for me, and every night he would commend me to God. I was wild and reckless and didn't like the restraint of home. When my father died, my mother took up the family worship. Many times she came to me and said, 'Oh, son, if you would stay for family worship, I would be the happiest mother on earth; but when I pray, you don't even stay in the house.'

"Sometimes I would go in at midnight from a night of drinking and hear my mother praying for me. Sometimes in the early hours of the morning I would hear her voice pleading for me. At last I felt that I must either become a Christian or leave home, and one day I gathered a few things together and stole away from home without letting my mother know.

"Sometime after, I heard indirectly that my mother was sick. Ah, I thought, it is my conduct that is making her ill! My first impulse was to go home and cheer her last days, but the thought came that if I did, I would have to become a Christian. My proud heart revolted and I said, "No, I will not become a Christian."

Months passed by, and he heard that his mother was worse. Then he thought, *If my mother does not live, I could never forgive myself.*

That thought took him home. He reached the old

village about dark, and started on foot for his home, which was about a mile and a half away. On the way he passed the graveyard and decided to go to his father's grave to see if there was a newly made grave beside it. As he approached the spot, his heart began to beat faster. When he got near enough, the light of the moon shone on a newly made grave, where he saw his mother's name on the headstone.

With a great deal of emotion, he continued speaking to the men at the YMCA: "Young men, for the first time in my life, this question came over me: Who is going to pray for my lost soul now? Father is gone and Mother is gone, and they are the only two who ever cared for me. If I could have called my mother back that night and heard her breathe my name in prayer, I would have given the world if it had been mine to give. I spent all that night by her grave, and God for Christ's sake heard my mother's prayers, and I became a child of God. But I never forgave myself for the way I treated my mother, and I never will."

Where is My Wandering Boy Tonight?

Where is my wandering boy tonight,
　　The boy of my tenderest care,
The boy that was once my joy and light,
　　The child of my love and prayer?

Once he was pure as morning dew,
    As he knelt at his mother's knee;
No face was so bright, no heart more true,
    And none was so sweet as he.

O, could I see you now, my boy,
    As fair as in olden time,
When prattle and smile made home a joy,
    And life was a merry chime.

Go for my wandering boy tonight,
    Go, search for him where you will;
But bring him to me with all his blight,
    And tell him I love him still.
       – Robert Lowry

My dear friends, God may forgive you, but the consequences of your sin are going to be bitter, even if you are forgiven.

A few years ago I was preaching in Chicago on the text, *Arise, go up to Bethel and dwell there* (Genesis 35:1). After the meeting, a man asked to see me alone, so we went into a private room. The perspiration stood in beads on his forehead.

I asked him, "What is it?"

He replied, "I am a fugitive from justice. I am in exile, in disguise. The government of my state has offered a reward for me. I have been hidden here for months. They tell me there is no hell, but it seems as though I have been in hell for months."

He had been a businessman, and having, as he

thought, plenty of money, he forged some bonds, thinking that he could give his check any time and call them in, but he got in over his head and fell. He said, "I have been here for six months. I have a wife and three children, but I cannot write to them or hear from them." The poor man was in terrible mental agony.

I said, "Why don't you go back, give yourself up, face the law, and ask God to forgive you?"

He said, "I would take the first train tomorrow and give myself up, except for one thing: I have a wife and three children – how can I bring disgrace upon them?"

I, too, have a wife and three children, and when he said that, the situation seemed very different.

Ah! If we could do our own reaping, it would not be so bitter, but when we make our little children, or our wife, or our old, gray-haired mother, or our old father reap with us, isn't the reaping pretty bitter? I don't fear any pestilence or any disease as much as I fear sin. If God will only keep sin out of my family, I will praise Him in time and in eternity. The worst enemy that ever crossed a person's path is sin.

If a person comes to me for advice, I always try to put myself in the place of the one to whom I am talking, and then I try to give the best advice I can. I said to this man, "I don't know what to say, but it is safe to pray."

After I had prayed, I urged him to pray, but he said, "If I do, it means the penitentiary."

I asked him to come the next day at twelve noon. He met me at the appointed hour and said, "It is all settled. If I ever want to meet the God of Bethel, I must go through the prison to meet Him. God helping me, I will give myself up. I am going back, and I would like to have you keep quiet until I give myself over into the hands of the law; then you can hold me up as a warning. Little did I think when I started out in life that I was coming to this! Little did I think when I married a girl from one of the first families in the state that I would bring such disgrace on her."

At four o'clock that afternoon he went back to Missouri. He reached home a little past midnight and spent a week with his family. In a letter he said that he didn't dare let his children know he was there, lest they tell the neighbor's children. At night he would sneak out and look at his children, but he couldn't take them in his arms or kiss them. Oh, there is the result of sin! Would to God that every one of us would just turn from sin today!

One day when this man was in hiding, he heard his little boy ask, "Mama, doesn't Papa love us anymore?"

"Yes," his mother replied. "Why do you ask?"

"Well," the little fellow said, "he has been gone so long and he never writes us any letters and never comes to see us."

The last night he came out from hiding and took a long look at those innocent, sleeping children. Then he took his wife and kissed her again and again, and leaving that once happy home, he gave himself up to the sheriff. The next morning he pleaded guilty and was sent to the penitentiary for nineteen years. I believe that God had forgiven him, but he couldn't forgive himself, and he had to reap what he sowed. I pleaded with the governor for mercy, and the man was pardoned.

Some time ago I was telling this story, and someone doubted it, but the governor who pardoned him happened to be in the meeting. He rose and said, "I pardoned that man myself." The governor pardoned him, and he lived a few years, but from the time he committed that sin, he had to reap what he had sowed. Oh, reader, I plead with you: overcome your besetting sin, whatever it is!

Future Punishment

I can imagine someone saying, "I am glad Mr. Moody hasn't tried to scare us about the future state. I agree with him that we will receive all our reward and punishment in this life."

If you think I believe that, you are greatly mistaken. One sentence from the lips of the Son of God in regard to the future state has forever settled it in my mind: *Ye shall die in your sins; where I go, ye shall not be able to come* (John 8:21). If a man has not given up his drunkenness, his profanity, his immorality, and his covetousness, heaven would be hell to him. Heaven is a prepared place for prepared people. What would a person do in heaven who cannot bear to be in the society of the pure and holy down here?

It is not true that all reward and punishment is reaped in this life. Look how many crimes are committed in which the perpetrators are never caught. It often happens that the worst criminal uses his experience to escape detection, while someone less criminally minded is captured. A man ruins a girl. Does he always reap punishment here? No. He holds his head as high as ever in society, while the unfortunate victim of his lust who, perhaps, was innocently beguiled into sin by him, becomes an outcast. His punishment, however, is at best only postponed to another world.

Eternity!

Oh, the clanging bells of Time!
    Night and day they never cease;
We are wearied with their chime,
    For they do not bring us peace;
And we hush our breath to hear,
    And we strain our eyes to see
If thy shores are drawing near –
    Eternity! Eternity!

Oh, the clanging bells of Time!
    How their changes rise and fall,
But in undertone sublime,
    Sounding clearly through them all,
Is a voice that must be heard,
    As our moments onward flee,
And it speaketh, aye, one word –
    Eternity! Eternity!

Oh, the clanging bells of Time!
   To their voices, loud and low,
In a long, unresting line
   We are marching to and fro;
And we yearn for sight or sound,
   Of the life that is to be,
For thy breath doth wrap us round –
   Eternity! Eternity!

Oh, the clanging bells of Time!
   Soon their notes will all be dumb,
And in joy and peace sublime
   We shall feel the silence come;
And our souls their thirst will slake,
   And our eyes the King will see,
When thy glorious morn shall break –
   Eternity! Eternity!
            – Ellen M H. Gates

Chapter 8

Warning

Take heed that no one deceive you.
(Matthew 24:4)

Christ in you, the hope of glory, whom we preach, warning every man and teaching in all wisdom that we may present every man perfect in Christ Jesus. (Colossians 1:27-28)

To give a warning is a sign of love. Who warns like a mother, and who loves like a mother? Your mother, perhaps, is gone, and maybe your father is gone. Let me take the place of those who have departed, and let me lift up a warning voice. With Paul I would say, *I do not write these things to shame you, but to warn you, as to my beloved sons* (1 Corinthians 4:14).

A pilot guiding a steamer down the Cumberland River saw a light, apparently from a small craft, in the middle of the narrow channel. His impulse was to disregard the signal and run down the boat. As he came near, a voice shouted, "Keep off! Keep off!"

In great anger he cursed whom he thought was a boatman in his way. On arriving at his next landing, he learned that a huge rock had fallen from the mountain into the bed of the stream, and a signal had been placed there to warn the coming boats of the unknown danger. Alas! Many regard God's warnings in the same way, and they are angry with anyone who tells them about the rocks in their course. They will understand better at the end.

The children of Israel had no truer friend than Moses. They never went astray without him warning them, and trouble never came upon them except when his warnings were unheeded. Elijah was the best friend Ahab had.

I wish I could warn as Jesus Christ did. As He went up the Mount of Olives, His heart seemed to be greatly moved, and He cried, *O Jerusalem, Jerusalem, which kills the prophets and stones those that are sent unto thee, how often would I have gathered thy children together as a hen gathers her brood under her wings, and ye would not!* (Luke 13:34). Did He not warn people?

If a friend of mine were about to invest in a worthless silver mine, do you think I would be true to him if I did not warn him against it? Do I show less love for him because I warn him against actions that will bring a harvest of misery and despair? *Then whoever hears the sound of the shofar and does not take warning; and the coming of the sword should take him away, his blood shall be upon his own head. He heard the sound of the shofar and did not take warning; his blood shall be upon himself. But he that takes warning shall deliver his soul* (Ezekiel 33:4-5).

Be sure that the seed you are sowing is good seed. If you sow to the flesh, a good harvest will be impossible. Good seed and bad seed cannot both succeed if allowed to grow together. One prospers at the expense of the other, and the likelihood is that the bad seed will get the upper hand. Weeds always seem to grow and spread more rapidly than good seed.

The longer they live, the firmer hold the weeds gain. Delay is dangerous. In the year 1691, a proclamation was sent throughout the Highlands of Scotland that everyone who had been guilty of rebellion against the established government would be pardoned if, before the last day of the year, he laid down his arms and promised to end his rebellion. Many did so, but one chief named Maclan put off submission from week to week, always intending to submit before it was too late. When at last he started out to accept the pardon, he was hindered by a great storm and did not arrive until the time had expired. The day of pardon had passed, and the day of vengeance had come. Maclan and his men were put to death.

> Good seed and bad seed cannot both succeed if allowed to grow together.

It is wise to exterminate the weeds at once. Beware of remaining longer in sin. The deeper you sink, the more bitter will be your restoration. Why continue to sear your conscience and sow the seeds of bitter remorse? No matter how painful it may be, break with sin at once! Serious operations are often necessary when the skillful surgeon knows that the disease cannot be cured by surface applications. The farmer takes his hoe and his spade and his axe, and he cuts away the troublesome growths and burns the roots out of the ground with fire.

> *Therefore if thy right eye should bring thee occasion to stumble, pluck it out and cast it from thee; for it is better for thee that one of thy members should perish, and not that thy whole body should be cast into hell. And if thy right hand should bring thee occasion to stumble, cut it off, and cast it from thee: for it is better for thee that one of thy members should perish, and not that thy whole body should be cast into hell.* (Matthew 5:29-30)

Remember that the tares and the wheat will be separated at the judgment day, if not before. Sowing to the flesh and sowing to the Spirit inevitably lead to diverging paths (Galatians 6:8). *The axe is laid unto the root of the trees; every tree therefore which does not bring forth good fruit is hewn down and cast into the fire* (Luke 3:9). *He will thoroughly purge his threshing floor and will gather the wheat into his storehouse, but the chaff he will burn with fire unquenchable* (Luke 3:17). Beware of your habits.

A recent writer has said:

> Could the young but realize how soon they will become mere walking bundles of habits,

they would give more heed to their conduct while in the [moldable] state. We are spinning our own fates, good or evil, and never to be undone. Every smallest stroke of virtue or of vice leaves its never so little scar. The drunken Rip Van Winkle, in Jefferson's play, excuses himself for every fresh dereliction by saying, "I won't count this time!" Well! He may not count it, and a kind Heaven may not count it; but it is being counted none the less. Down among his nerve cells and fibers the molecules are counting it, registering and storing it up, to be used against him when the next temptation comes.

Nothing we ever do is, in strict scientific literalness, wiped out. Of course, this has its good side as well as its bad one. As we become permanent drunkards by so many separate drinks, so we become saints in the moral [sphere], and authorities and experts in the practical and scientific spheres, by so many separate acts and hours of work.[5]

Beware of temptations. *Lead us not into temptation* (Matthew 6:13), our Lord taught us to pray; and again He said, *Watch and pray, that ye enter not into temptation* (Matthew 26:41). We are weak and sinful by nature, and it is a good deal better for us to pray for deliverance from temptation rather than for strength

---

5 From *The Principles of Psychology*, by William James (1842-1910), an American philosopher and psychologist.

to resist when temptation has overtaken us. Prevention is better than cure. Hidden under the soil may be seeds of passion and wickedness that only wait for a favorable opportunity to shoot up. Young men pretend that it is necessary to see both sides of life. What foolishness! I am not called upon to put my hand in the fire to see if it will burn.

A steamboat was stranded on the Mississippi River, and the captain could not get her off. Eventually, a tough-looking fellow came on board and said, "Captain, I understand you need a pilot to get you out of this difficulty."

The captain asked, "Are you a pilot?"

"Well, they call me one."

"Do you know where the snags and sandbars are?"

"No, sir."

"Well, how do you expect to take me out of here if you don't know where the snags and sandbars are?"

"I know where they ain't!" was the satisfactory reply.

Begin to sow the good seed while the children are young, and thus prevent the weeds from getting a start. Satan does not wait until they grow up, and neither should we.

There are many fishing nets constructed so as to allow only full-grown fish to be caught, while the young can escape. Satan has nothing like that. He catches everything he can – the weakest and the strongest, the youngest and the oldest.

"We must care for our boys or the devil will," said a young Sunday school teacher.

"The devil will care for them anyway," answered the

old superintendent. "The devil will not neglect them, even if we do."

It is a masterpiece of the devil to make us believe that children cannot understand Christianity. Would Jesus have made a child the standard of faith if He had known that the child was not capable of understanding His words? It is far easier for children to love and trust than for grown-ups, so we should set Christ before them as the supreme object of their choice.

Do not neglect opportunities. Napoleon used to say, "There is a crisis in every battle – ten or fifteen minutes – on which the issue of the battle depends. To gain this is victory; to lose it is defeat."

Beware of sin. Its wages are death, and as has been said, the wages have never been reduced. Sin deceives people as to the satisfaction to be found in it, the excuses to be made for it, and the certainty of the punishment that must follow. If it was not deceitful, it would never be delightful. It comes in innocently and saps the lifeblood, depriving people of the moral capacity to do good.

Canon Wilberforce, walking in the Isle of Skye in Scotland, saw a magnificent golden eagle soaring upward. He stopped and watched its flight. He soon observed that something was wrong. It began to fall, and it soon lay dead at his feet. Eager to know the reason for its death, he examined it and found no trace of a gunshot wound, but he saw in its talons a small weasel, which, in its flight, had drawn near the eagle's body and sucked the lifeblood from the eagle's breast. Such is the end of everyone who persistently clings to sin.

Do not be deceived by the attractiveness of this world. It will cheat you and destroy you. The *Redoutable* was the name of a French ship that Lord Nelson twice spared from destruction, and it was from the rigging of that very ship that the fatal ball that killed him was fired. The devil administers many sins in honey, but there is poison mixed in with it. The truest pleasures spring from the good seed of righteousness; none else are profitable.

Beware of ignorance and indifference. You cannot afford to neglect your soul. There is too much at stake. I never knew a frivolous man to be converted. Until he wakes up and realizes his lost and hopeless condition, God Almighty will not reach down and take him by the hand. A ship was once in great danger at sea, and all were on their knees except one man. They called to him to come and join them in prayer, but he replied, "Not me. It's your business to look after the ship. I'm only a passenger."

Remember that mere knowledge is not enough. Many people know the gospel doctrine and promises by heart who are not touched by saving grace. Knowledge is often useless and can even be harmful, and what we need is to know God's will and observe it. Even good resolutions are not enough. No doubt they are helpful in their own way, but the Bible does not lead us to believe that they can save anyone. It does not say, "As many as resolved to receive him, to them gave he power to become the sons of God, even to them that resolve to believe on his name," but it says, *As many as received him, to them gave he power to become sons of God, even to them that believe on his name* (John 1:12).

Be watchful! There is constant need to be on guard so that we do not fall into sin. "Set a double guard upon that point tonight," was the command of a prudent officer when an attack was expected. At best, there will be some tares among the wheat. We all carry around with us material that Satan can work on. Paul said:

> *I know that in me (that is, in my flesh) dwells no good thing; for I have the desire, but I am not able to perform that which is good. For I do not do the good that I desire; but the evil which I do not desire, that I do. And if I do that which I do not desire, I am not working, but sin that dwells in me. So that, desiring to do good, I find this law: evil is natural unto me. For I delight with the law of God with the inward man, but I see another law in my members which rebels against the law of my mind, bringing captive unto the law of sin which is in my members. O wretched man that I am! who shall deliver me from the body of this death?* (Romans 7:18-24)

Blessed be God that he could add, *Who shall deliver me from the body of this death? The grace of God, by Jesus, the Christ, our Lord.* (Romans 7:25).

The issue that God has placed before us is clear-cut: *He that believes in the Son has eternal life, and he that does not obey the Son shall not see life, but the wrath of God abides on him* (John 3:36). There is no middle course: *he that believes,* or *he that does not obey.* He leaves us to choose, and the responsibility rests upon us.

It might cost you much sacrifice and twist many heartstrings to make the right choice, but I plead with you to take the decisive step now. The salvation of your soul outweighs all other considerations. Will you risk your eternity for the sake of some present gain or pleasure? Bow your head and pray, "Heavenly Father, I now choose to come unto You as a poor, humble sinner. I believe on Your Son, whom You sent to be my Savior. Trusting in the merits of His blood, which was shed as a propitiation for my sins, I rest in the assurance of sins forgiven."

Will you risk your eternity for the sake of some present gain or pleasure?

There is hope for the most wicked sinner. Wherever weeds grow, there is the possibility of good seed growing. The greater your need, the more welcome you will be to Jesus. He knows the proud and the self-confident afar off, but the faintest whisper of the contrite sinner commands His attention.

Our Lord gave us a simple test to help us in our choice. He said, *For a good tree does not bring forth corrupt fruit; neither does a corrupt tree bring forth good fruit. For every tree is known by its own fruit* (Luke 6:43-44). Many of us do not have the time or ability to unravel intricate arguments or grasp profound doctrines. Certain phases of truth are often inaccessible to the ordinary mind, but the test Christ gave is short and practical, and it is within the reach of any of us.

"Have you ever heard the gospel?" a missionary asked a Chinese man whom he had not seen in his mission before.

"No," he replied, "but I have seen it. I know a man who used to be the terror of his neighborhood. He was a bad opium smoker and was as dangerous as a wild beast, but he completely changed. He is now gentle and good and has stopped smoking opium."

Apply this test to unbelief. What are its fruits? Crime follows in its track. Society becomes disorganized. Chastity, honesty, and the other virtues are undermined. All of life becomes messed up.

The following brief extract from a letter written in an English prison is a tremendous arraignment of that system of belief that does not acknowledge God: "I am one of thirteen unbelievers. Where are my friends? Four have been hanged. One became a Christian. Six have been sentenced to various terms of imprisonment, and one is now confined in a cell above me, sentenced to life in prison."

With all reverence, we can apply this text to our Lord Himself. We have His own authority for it. On one occasion when the Jews objected to His actions, He said, *The works which the Father has given me to finish, the same works that I do, bear witness of me that the Father has sent me* (John 5:36).

On another occasion they gathered around Him and said:

*Until when wilt thou hold our soul in sus-
pense? If thou art the Christ, tell us plainly.*

*Jesus answered them, I have told you, and
ye do not believe; the works that I do in my
Father's name, they bear witness of me. . . .
If I do not do the works of my Father, do not
believe me. But if I do, though ye do not
believe me, believe the works that ye may
know and believe that the Father is in me and
I in him.* (John 10:24-25, 37-38)

Nicodemus had good reason to say, *Rabbi, we know
that thou art a teacher come from God, for no one can
do these signs that thou doest unless God is with him*
(John 3:2). Also, Peter said, *Ye men of Israel, hear these
words: Jesus of Nazareth, a man approved of God among
you by miracles and wonders and signs, which God did
by him in the midst of you, as ye yourselves also know*
(Acts 2:22).

What are the fruits of extravagance, pride, and covetousness? On the other hand, what are the fruits of
prayer, fearing God, and doing His commandments?
What are the fruits of heathenism? Look at Africa,
China, India, and the islands of the seas with their gods
of wood and stone. What must be the intelligence and
moral sense of people who will worship such things?

Even the best of non-Christian religions must always
prove to be a failure. It cannot be denied that many
of the highest virtues are encouraged in the writings
of heathen philosophers. How could it be otherwise?

Morality is as universal as humanity, and it is only to be expected that every once in a while some thinking person would move beyond the average and read deeper into the foundational truths of ethics. In my mind, this fact only proves the intimate connection between the human and the divine. Christianity never claimed to introduce a brand-new system of morality.

Will these non-Christian religions bear the test? Stoicism was perhaps the noblest of the Greek philosophies, but it rapidly developed into utter cynicism and culminated in the stated impossibility of being able to become virtuous. Epicureanism started out fairly well, but its founder was not even dead before it earned for itself the disgraceful epithet that it was a doctrine worthy only of swine. Look at Buddhism, with its filthy ceremonies and cruel tortures. All these systems show a conflict between theory and practice. They failed in their objective because they approached the difficulty in the wrong way. They trimmed away at the branch, not recognizing that the tree was rotten at heart.

Christianity alone will stand the test of raising mankind out of the pit. How does it propose to do so? Not by minimizing the danger and need. The Bible says, *Every head is sick, and every heart faint. From the sole of the foot even unto the head there is no soundness in him; but wounds, and bruises, and putrefying sores* (Isaiah 1:5-6). Christianity demands a new birth, regeneration by the Holy Spirit, as the first thing needed: *Ye must be born again* (John 3:7). Christianity does not place sanctification before justification, but it first imparts life from above, and then it envelops the redeemed sinner in the love of Christ and the fellowship and guidance of the Holy Spirit.

A converted Chinese man once told about his experience:

> I was down in a deep pit, half sunk in the mire, crying for someone to help me out. I looked up and saw a venerable, gray-haired man looking down at me.
>
> "My son," he said, "this is a dreadful place."
>
> "Yes," I answered. "I fell into it; can't you help me out?"
>
> "My son," was his reply, "I am Confucius. If you had read my books and followed what they taught, you would never have been here."
>
> "Yes, father," I said, "but can't you help me out?"
>
> As I looked up, he was gone. I soon saw another form approaching me, and then another man leaned over me, this time with closed eyes and folded arms. He seemed to be looking to some far-off place.
>
> "My son," Buddha said, "just close your eyes and fold your arms, and forget all about yourself. Get into a state of rest. Don't think about anything that can disturb you. Get so still that nothing can move you. Then, my

child, you will be in such delightful rest as I am."

"Yes, father," I answered. "I will when I am above ground. Can't you help me out?" But Buddha, too, was gone.

I was just beginning to sink into despair when I saw another figure above me, different from the others. There were marks of suffering on His face. I cried out to Him, "O, Father! Can you help me?"

"My child," He said, "what is the matter?"

Before I could answer Him, He was down in the mire by my side. He folded His arms about me and lifted me up; then He fed me and allowed me to rest. When I was well, He did not say, "Now, don't do that again," but He said, "We will walk on together now" – and we have been walking together ever since.

This was a poor Chinese man's way of telling of the compassionate love and help of the Lord Jesus.

I was reading some time ago about a young man who had just come out of a saloon and had mounted his horse. As a certain deacon passed by on his way to church, the young man followed him and asked, "Deacon, can you tell me how far it is to hell?"

The deacon's heart was pained to think that a young man like that should talk so lightly about eternity. He passed on by and said nothing. When he came around the corner to the church, he saw that the horse had thrown that young man, and he was dead. So you may be nearer the judgment than you think.

When I was in Switzerland many years ago, I learned some solemn lessons about the suddenness with which death can overtake us. I saw several places where landslides had occurred, completely destroying whole villages. I saw where avalanches had swept down the mountainsides, leaving destruction in their wake.

A terrible calamity happened in the year 1806 to a village called Goldau, situated in a fertile valley at the foot of the Rossberg Mountain. The season had been unusually wet, and this had made the crops all the more abundant. Early one morning a young peasant, passing the cottage of an old man whom he knew, saw him sitting at the door in the full rays of the sun.

"Good morning, neighbor," he said. "We are likely to have a fine day."

"It's about time that we have a fine day," growled the old man. "It has been wet enough lately."

"Have you heard the report?" asked the other. "Those who were up the earliest this morning declare they saw the top of old Rossberg move."

"Indeed! It is likely enough," said the old man. "Mark my words, and I have often said it before: I won't live to see it, but those who are now young will not live to be as old as I am before the top of that mountain lies at its foot."

"I hope it will not be in my day," said the young man, and he passed on, little thinking how near the prediction was to being fulfilled, and that the ripening fields of corn and the abundant clusters of luscious grapes would never be gathered; but so it was.

The springs of water in the mountain had been overcharged by the excessive rains, and these, in forcing their way to the surface and toward the valley below, had loosened the masses of rounded rock that had been cemented together by a kind of clay, of which material the upper part of the mountain was formed. These huge masses at length gave way and fell headlong into the valley, burying the entire village and about eight hundred of its inhabitants beneath their weight.

What became of the old man? Sadly, he did not escape. He believed the mountain would fall, but he did not think the fall was near. He was sitting in his cottage, contentedly smoking his pipe, when the young man came back quickly, crying out, "The mountain is falling!"

The old man calmly rose from his seat, looked out his door, and said, "I will have time to fill my pipe again," and he went back into his house. The young man was saved. The old man perished before he had left his cottage. It and its owner were crushed and swept to the bottom of the valley.

I was in the north of England in 1881 when a fearful storm swept over that part of the country. A great many of the fishermen attended the congregation of a friend of mine who was a minister at Eyemouth. It had been very stormy weather, and the fishermen had been detained in the harbor for a week. One day, however, the sun shone out in a clear blue sky. It seemed as if the storm had passed away, and the boats started out for the fishing ground. Forty-one boats left the harbor that day. Before they started, the harbormaster hoisted the storm signal and warned them of an approaching storm. He begged them not to go, but they disregarded his warning, and away they went. They saw no sign of the coming storm. In a few hours, however, it swept down on that coast, and very few of those fishermen returned. There were five or six men in each boat, and nearly all were lost in that dreadful gale. In the church of which my friend was pastor, I believe there were only three male members left.

Those men were ushered into eternity because they did not give heed to the warning. I lift up the storm signal now and warn you to escape from the coming judgment!

There was a man living near one of the main highways a number of years ago, who one night saw that a landside had obstructed the train track. He saw by the clock that he didn't have time to reach the telegraph office to stop the night express, so he grabbed a lantern and started up the track, thinking he might be in time to stop the train. As he was running, he fell, and the light in his lantern went out. He didn't have another match, and he could hear the train coming in the distance. He didn't know what to do. As a last resort he stood on the bank, and the moment the train came near enough to him, he hurled the lantern with all his might at the engineer.

Make up your mind now that by the grace of God you will obtain the victory.

The engineer saw that something must be wrong, took the warning, applied the brakes, and stopped the train within a few yards of the obstruction.

I throw the broken lantern at your feet now! I beg you to take warning and make a clean break from sin, no matter what it may cost you. Take warning! You must give up sin, or you must give up the hope of heaven. Put yourself in the way of being blessed. Make up your mind now that by the grace of God you will obtain the victory.

> *Let the wicked forsake his way, and the unrighteous man his thoughts: and let him return unto the Lord, and he will have mercy upon him; and to our God, for he will abundantly pardon* (Isaiah 55:7).

Dwight L. Moody –
A Brief Biography

Dwight Lyman Moody was born on February 5, 1837, in Northfield, Massachusetts. His father died when Dwight was only four years old, leaving his mother with nine children to care for. When Dwight was seventeen years old, he left for Boston to work as a salesman. A year later, he was led to Jesus Christ by Edward Kimball, Moody's Sunday school teacher. Moody soon left for Chicago and began teaching a Sunday school class of his own. By the time he was twenty-three, he had become a successful shoe salesman, earing $5,000 in only eight months, which was a lot of money for the middle of the nineteenth century. Having decided to follow Jesus, though, he left his career to engage in Christian work for only $300 a year.

D. L. Moody was not an ordained minister, but was an effective evangelist. He was once told by Henry Varley, a British evangelist, "Moody, the world has yet to see what God will do with a man fully consecrated to Him."

Moody later said, "By God's help, I aim to be that man."

It is estimated that during his lifetime, without the help of television or radio, Moody traveled more than one million miles, preached to more than one million people, and personally dealt with over seven hundred and fifty thousand individuals.

D. L. Moody died on December 22, 1899.

Moody once said, "Some day you will read in the papers that D. L. Moody, of East Northfield, is dead. Don't you believe a word of it! At that moment I shall be more alive than I am now. I shall have gone up higher, that is all – out of this old clay tenement into a house that is immortal; a body that death cannot touch, that sin cannot taint, a body fashioned like unto His glorious body. I was born of the flesh in 1837. I was born of the Spirit in 1856. That which is born of the flesh may die. That which is born of the Spirit will live forever."

Similar Updated Classics

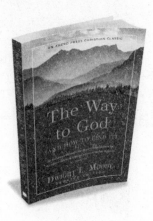

The Way to God, by Dwight L. Moody

There is life in Christ. Rich, joyous, wonderful life. It is true that the Lord disciplines those whom He loves and that we are often tempted by the world and our enemy, the devil. But if we know how to go beyond that temptation to cling to the cross of Jesus Christ and keep our eyes on our Lord, our reward both here on earth and in heaven will be 100 times better than what this world has to offer.

This book is thorough. It brings to life the love of God, examines the state of the unsaved individual's soul, and analyzes what took place on the cross for our sins. *The Way to God* takes an honest look at our need to repent and follow Jesus, and gives hope for unending, joyous eternity in heaven.

Available where books are sold.

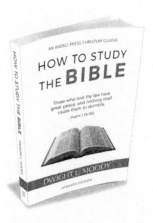

How to Study the Bible,
by Dwight L. Moody

There is no situation in life for which you cannot find some word of consolation in Scripture. If you are in affliction, if you are in adversity and trial, there is a promise for you. In joy and sorrow, in health and in sickness, in poverty and in riches, in every condition of life, God has a promise stored up in His Word for you.

This classic book by Dwight L. Moody brings to light the necessity of studying the Scriptures, presents methods which help stimulate excitement for the Scriptures, and offers tools to help you comprehend the difficult passages in the Scriptures. To live a victorious Christian life, you must read and understand what God is saying to you. Moody is a master of using stories to illustrate what he is saying, and you will be both inspired and convicted to pursue truth from the pages of God's Word.

Available where books are sold.

The Overcoming Life, by Dwight L. Moody

Are you an overcomer? Or, are you plagued by little sins that easily beset you? Even worse, are you failing in your Christian walk, but refuse to admit and address it? No Christian can afford to dismiss the call to be an overcomer. The earthly cost is minor; the eternal reward is beyond measure.

Dwight L. Moody is a master at unearthing what ails us. He uses stories and humor to bring to light the essential principles of successful Christian living. Each aspect of overcoming is looked at from a practical and understandable angle. The solution Moody presents for our problems is not religion, rules, or other outward corrections. Instead, he takes us to the heart of the matter and prescribes biblical, God-given remedies for every Christian's life. Get ready to embrace genuine victory for today, and joy for eternity.

Available where books are sold.

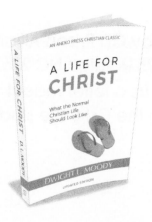

A Life for Christ, by Dwight L. Moody

In the church today, we have everything buttoned up perfectly. The music is flawless, the sermon well-prepared and smoothly delivered, and the grounds meticulously kept. People come on time and go home on time. But a fundamental element is missing. The business of church has undermined the individual's need to truly live for Christ, so much so, that only a limited few are seeing their life impact the world.

Dwight L. Moody takes us deep into Scripture and paints a clear picture of what ought to be an individual's life for Christ. The call for each Christian is to become an active member in the body of Christ. The motive is love for the Lord and our neighbor. The result will be the salvation of men, women, and children everywhere.

Available where books are sold.